PROFESSION

THE A

"Stirring and moving to the very core, each story and lesson resonates and is immediately useful. Never remove it from your desk; refer to it always."

*Charlotte Eulette, International Director,
Celebrant Foundation & Institute*

"Wow . . . you know how you have a handful of books that you always refer back to when you need centering? *The Art of Flow* is one of them. Its language and message is beautifully descriptive and brilliantly succinct. What a wonderful gift for any family, friends or client [feeling] stuck or overwhelmed."

*Tammy Tombroff. MSW, LCSW,
Lifestyle Counseling & Life Coach*

The author's "Flow" principles align themselves to Christian principles in such a way that I found myself reinforcing the old adage, "What would Jesus do?" . . . [It is] organized in short, concise chapters that are simple to understand, easy to remember, and directly actionable. I saw myself on many pages to one degree or another, and the exercises at the end of each chapter reinforce the life lessons learned.

I recommend this book to anyone that is interested in spiritual growth, with the understanding that with change being inevitable, how one handles it is the key to tranquility.

*TS Robinson
www.tsrbook.com*

THE ART *of* FLOW

THE PATH TO A TRANSFORMED LIFE

FREDDIE ZERINGUE, CHt

Published by Art of Flow Productions

The Art of Flow – The Path to a Transformed Life
First Edition

Copyright © 2013 Freddie Zeringue
Published by Art of Flow Productions

Print
ISBN-13: 978-0-9915931-0-1
ISBN-10: 0991593103

First printing March 2014

Visit the official Art of Flow® website at http://www.ArtofFlow.com for free supplemental materials and updates on upcoming releases.

*I dedicate this book to all the people who
have made this process possible.*

My mother, Nell D. Zeringue, for standing behind me while teaching me love and kindness, gentleness, and the ability to nurture and support others. It is in her memory and through her hard work, dedication and endurance that my passion for making a difference for others grows.

To my ex-wife Debra and my sons Kaleb and Zachary, for joining me on this lifelong journey of transformation and enduring with me through all that it has taken to get to this point. Without them none of this could be possible.

I want to thank and acknowledge Mica McPheeters, without whom this book might have never made it through the editing process. Mica is a special gift and this book embodies an extra-special love because she has been part of its evolution.

In addition, I would like to dedicate my works to God and all of the people I have had the honor and the privilege to work with over the years, including those who helped me along the way. You truly are the heroes in the story of my life. It is your willingness to include me in your lives that has made mine so rich with love and worth experiencing.

TABLE OF CONTENTS

HOW TO READ THIS BOOK

This book is intended to be an experiential journey designed to transform your life—ultimately creating the meaningful experience you always felt it could be. With that aim in mind, it has been written in a very specific way and is rich with examples illustrating applications of the principles being discussed. Certain themes appear in more than one chapter in order to reiterate concepts from different perspectives and enhance your overall understanding. While most books present you with information, I have included these applications of use in a real-world environment so that you can practice them on a daily basis. Do not take this lightly; if you skip incorporating them into your life you'll miss the point of the process. You'll get the most transformative benefits if you purposefully live with them in your consciousness, as opposed to having a mere conceptual understanding.

The ideal method to follow while reading this book is to absorb one chapter at a time. Read the content and do the accompanying exercises, then simply give yourself a day or two to embrace the material you've just covered. In most cases, I would suggest rereading a chapter after you've given it thought and time before going on to the next. As you progress through this book, you'll notice that it's not the dramatic awakenings or revelations that you're looking for, but the small, subtle points of enlightenment that begin to crystallize and create a larger experience, like fireflies softly gathering in the night air and illuminating a world you knew was within reach.

Take your time and follow the exercises at the end of each chapter; if possible, discuss the material you're digesting. As your paradigms shift and your comprehension changes, it can be helpful to have a sounding board. Talk about it with a friend or two, or better yet, read the book as a group. Being around others who have experienced the book provides reinforcement during transformative shifts and will support you as you grow, proving to amplify your insights while studying each topic.

Due to the spiritual nature of the book, parts of the text can become dense as you encounter concepts that uniquely challenge you to deepen your comprehension and alter your perceptions. During your own personal awakening, it may continue to reveal things to you as you evolve and find your *Art of Flow*. To put that statement into perspective, writing and editing this book has been a powerful experience for everyone associated with its development. The more often and deeply we delved into these principles during the editing process, the more new understandings we encountered—myself included. There is truly a power and veracity contained in these pages.

May your experience unveil the path of Flow and your breakthroughs lead you to a life filled with purpose and enlightenment.

FREE MATERIALS

This book is complemented by free audio recordings and additional publications that expound upon the Art of Flow topics you are about to explore. Visit the official website of the book for downloading instructions and for more information about upcoming releases and events.

OFFICIAL WEBSITE:

http://www.ArtofFlow.com

INTRODUCTION

As a personal coach and facilitator in the field of human development and transformation for more than 20 years, I have had the pleasure of working directly and indirectly with countless people. The concepts contained in this book are a direct result of the observations, experiences, and lessons I have learned during that process and in my own life. With a background in communications, hypnosis, and life design, I have been able to assimilate a group of concepts I refer to as *Flow* (a natural rhythm in life), which work together in a fluid dance I've termed the *Art of Flow*. The mastery of these concepts make it practical for anyone to live a life of non-resistance and intentional creation via the Universal Laws of Attraction, whereby life continually unfolds harmoniously in a peaceful and fulfilling manner.

In this text, you will find the essence of most self-help and self-development books on the market, including those on spiritual development. What you'll discover in this book, however, is a stripped-down version of most of their concepts and some simple, easy illustrations with personal examples. My goal is not to enlighten you, the reader, but to provide understanding that these universal principles are a set of tools that will equip you to bring forth personal enlightenment and transformation. It will require your own effort to do the work, because lasting enlightenment is truly a personal journey.

You'll learn as you move through this book that the concepts presented here are ancient, yet in a present day context they have the power to transform a person's life, giving them a new level of power and freedom. To achieve true happiness and experience inner peace, fulfillment, and freedom with a sense of purpose and well-being, an individual must reach a state of complete self-acceptance. Once self-acceptance is reached, it is possible to design one's life through intention and dance to the rhythm of the universe. The individual's need to prove themselves fades, ego loses its attachment to fixed ideas, and ideas no longer hold them back in life . . . They reach a state of fluidity.

As you read and apply these concepts, know that my heart is with you in Spirit. My personal wish for you is that you find the vortex of transformation that is contained in these pages and pass through it to a new happiness and freedom. Know that I hold for you a space that contains all the blessings of the Universe!

STORY OF THE BOOK

As I looked into her eyes, peering through to her soul, I saw a reflection of me as part of her, her as part of me and us as part of all that is, ever was and ever will be. Her face now 10 years younger in appearance, her smile radiant and bold, she barely resembled the friend who walked into my home for a personal retreat from life just 24 hours before. It was in that moment I realized how much I had missed doing transformational work as a personal coach.

My friend suggested that I should open a place where people could come for an individual coaching retreat with me and experience the things she had. We spoke about how cool it would be to have a location where individuals in despair could find a haven from the world for a weekend, receiving guidance on their life journey and personal path of enlightenment.

At one point, she suggested a book. I told her I had tried to write books in the past, but it never worked out. I explained that each time I tried to write down the concepts, the resulting content was very brief. In fact, I told her that if I wrote a book, it would probably only be about 25 pages long and contain essentially the same principles as 90 percent of the self-development and spiritual books on the market—an idea that seemed absurd to me. She disagreed and encouraged me to do it right away.

After she left, I found my mind filled with thoughts of a center—preferably a houseboat. It was a lifelong dream of mine to live on a large houseboat where I could have people over to do retreats and transformational work. Then I thought more about a book. The next morning, I found myself putting down some of the very concepts that I convey in coaching sessions. I was amazed at how perfect it felt to write with no expectations of producing a lengthy book—just a few simple notes to convey some concepts I use when doing transformational work.

Shortly after I finished that day, I went to pick up my teenage son. We got home and I walked into the room where my office manager was working. While I was talking to her, I had an incredibly intense pain slowly move into my chest. I staggered to my chair and sat down. As a result of serious injuries incurred when I was much younger, pain is not new for me or the people around me. She thought it was my back, as usual, until I explained I thought I could be having a heart attack. The problem is that because of some of the injuries, I have no way to know for sure.

I had plans that day and didn't want to go to the doctor. The second wave was even more intense, but then subsided quickly. Only a week before, I had become a grandfather for the first time, and my first thought was of my grandson. My second thought was of my children, especially the one still living at home with me who was witnessing this event. Suddenly, I was fine. However, the scare really lingered in my mind. After that event and for the rest of the day, I thought of nothing but transformational work and how much I could contribute on the subject. I thought about what I would like to convey and how important it is to me to empower others toward personal transformation.

That evening I went to bed and had a very difficult night. I kept waking up to dreams that dealt with me leaving this world—flashes of the things I've accomplished and various completion work (workshops and processes I'd done to resolve issues and unfinished events in my life) with the ones I love. I felt like I was tying up loose ends before I left this world. What a shock! I had not anticipated this would occur. When I got up, all I could think about was writing this little book.

I've faced death many times in my life and it never bothered me before. I came to the conclusion that what bothered me wasn't the prospect of death, but the prospect of life and the passion that was reignited in me by working with my friend that weekend. She had awakened a mission within me to accomplish this book, and I didn't want to leave here without writing it. The realization that time could end at any moment inspired me to make it a priority. I viewed this as my personal awakening to a new chapter in life . . . each of us has many awakenings along the path of life, and this was one of mine.

I was simply not ready to die, and I wanted to share what I had to offer. These chapters are my adventure into new areas of growth and awakenings along my journey.

Enjoy the ride.

THE MASTER IN TRAINING

- a parable -

There once lived a young man who aspired to be a great Master. As he grew, he spent much of his time developing his relationship with Spirit and the Great Universe, and studying under men of great wisdom close to his home. He also faced many difficult experiences, but his bouts with adversity gave him great clarity concerning human existence and life.

Soon, many people came to him to glean the wisdom that he accumulated. Although he generously shared all he had learned, the Master-in-training still faced personal obstacles that were difficult to overcome. From the time he had been a small child, he had found it nearly impossible to remain silent and still, a tendency that continued to challenge him. He vocalized his thoughts constantly, and many questioned his wisdom because he could not live a life of quietness. "Surely, all Masters listen more than they speak," they would say. For many years, he lived with their judgments while continuing to share with those who sought his teachings.

After many years of resistance, one day he began to judge himself for speaking so profusely. He was convinced that the rest of the world must surely be right about him. How could a true Master be so talkative? He knew that he listened well and was a great observer, based on the feedback from his students, but still he suffered, wondering at his inability to live in quiet contemplation like other Masters.

Out of sheer frustration, he decided that he should travel to a distant land to learn from a Great Seer. His objective was to become as quiet outside as he felt inside.

He found sitting in the circle among the other students to be quite wonderful, and yet he heard nothing to aid his dilemma. At times, the Great Seer would be at a loss for words, uncertain how to answer a questioning student. It was then he would call upon his other pupils, and for each case, the Master-in-training would speak up. Words flowed from his lips like the waters of a stream, washing away the enigma and soothing his questioning peers. With much favor, the Seer began to call upon him repeatedly. Despite this, the Master-in-training was still frustrated at his inability to remain silent.

When the time came to leave the school of the Great Seer, the young man felt himself to be a failure. Even among the other young masters, he had been ridiculed for his constant dialogue. As he walked sadly through the garden that final morning, he crossed paths with the Great Seer. The Seer paused to consider the young man, and gazing deep into his eyes, instructed him, "Never cease what you do." The young Master was speechless. The Great Seer elaborated, saying, "You are perfectly matched with what you do; your skillful speech has the power to heal others. You speak that which others can only give thought to, you explain in words that which others can only feel, and you communicate that which you observe. You listen in a way that brings peace and joy. Your speech and its abundance are your realm of mastery. You are truly a Master.

Bidding the Seer goodbye, the young Master walked away with a quiet smile, having discovered his own level of mastery in the acceptance of what he thought to be his greatest defect.

THE AWAKENING

- chapter one -

*The path to enlightenment, freedom, and peace is filled
with a series of awakenings.*

Awakening is the process of becoming aware—aware of who and
what we are, and aware of what is truly taking place around us. The
process of awakening reveals hidden motivations, new possibilities, inherent strengths, and our ability to choose in life. Unfortunately, most of
us operate in a state of somnambulism—a fog of detachment—living our
lives out of habit and missing out on much of what life has to offer.

For the most part, we simply follow our routines—living "asleep at
the wheel" and therefore repeatedly struggling with the same core issues. These core issues crop up in our lives again and again through people, situations, and conditions—perhaps in different ways, but always
with the same underlying lessons waiting to be addressed. We continue
to run into the same walls—exhausting ourselves and causing tremendous stress on a daily basis. Most people carry around years of struggle
and strife from attempting to merely cope with their lives, feeling that
their burdens are becoming too much to bear.

With this in mind, where does the idea of conscious choice come in?
Perhaps a better question to ask ourselves should be, *"What keeps us from
experiencing freedom, peace, and growth?"*

Fortunately, we don't need to look very far. What stands in our way is
simply our own resistance to the change that life offers us each day—the
opportunity to redirect our conscious and unconscious efforts to protect
the **Ego**. *Our pain is in direct proportion to our resistance to change.* As the
well-known spiritual writer Emmet Fox stated in *Around the Year with
Emmet Fox,* "Change is the law of growth; growth is the law of life. That
which does not grow withers away and dies." Unfortunately, many people are just "withering away and dying," an unnatural state that causes
great pain and puts incredible demand on human beings from a physical, mental, and emotional standpoint. The eventual result is **emotional
collapse**, a humbling of the ego in order to let the light of day shine in. It

can be said that it's essential to die an internal death in order to be reborn into a new, awakened life.

What is it we're resisting? **We resist dealing with the unknown.**

As human beings, we're creatures of habit, and as creatures of habit, our survival mechanism tells us that change is bad—it is unknown. When faced with a point of crisis that demands change, the ego comes in and takes over. The ego does NOT like change because accepting change means that the current ideas of the ego must die and be replaced.

Resistance is the way of the ego, which uses the fight-or-flight system of survival to validate its campaign to prevent change, using linguistic fear as its weapon against the host. **Linguistic fears** arise from the language in our minds; they are imagined or ungrounded fears born of insecurities and conversations in our head. In many cases, we connect current conditions or conversations (internal or external dialogues) to past experiences, creating a distorted, fear-based story. The distortion of that story is usually derived from extreme circumstances and has the potential for great destruction.

If we look more closely, the unknown is actually a state of grace that produces the mindset of humility, or "no-mind." You're in constant flux and continually moving into unknown territory without all the answers, which has an uncanny side effect of adjusting your perspective. This highly desirable state is actually a springboard for great things to occur, notably an experience of awakening.

An awakening reflects a shift in consciousness; it creates a new presence and awareness in the current moment, empowering you to accept greater conscious choice in any or all areas of life. Awakening can happen in a flash or in can take years. It can occur in one area of your life at a time or shift your entire consciousness across all **domains**.

A useful example of this might be the cruise ship known as the World Residence. People who live on the World go to sleep in one country and wake up in an entirely different one the next day. Certain aspects of life have not changed, but others are altered dramatically. Residents still live on the ship, so their home has remained a constant, but the landscape and foods waiting to be experienced will be those of the destination country. If they venture off of the vessel, the culture they encounter will be notably distinct from what they found the day before. An awakening's effect on consciousness is much the same. You are still the same person physically, but everything around you takes on a different appearance.

Once an individual experiences an awakening, a complete rearrangement in perception occurs, bringing forth a heightened awareness in the domains that have been shifted. A person who was steeped in problems, drudgery, or negative behavior one minute discovers that all of their difficulties have begun to resolve to their greatest good the next—life begins to flow. From the depths of obscurity and confusion, a world of new possibilities emerges.

EXERCISE CONSCIOUSNESS

Review the ideas, patterns, and elements that you've held as true your entire life. Write them down as the absolutes that you have believed them to be. Next, take one and see if you can introduce an adjustment.

If you chose an idea, see if you can challenge that idea by researching an alternative view. Deeply consider all there is to know about that idea and its possibilities, but try not to be skewed by what you've always believed about it. Be open-minded and honestly look at it with fresh eyes.

Now review your own belief with the same research and attention. You'll probably notice just how little information your belief was based upon. It may be something you simply accepted from childhood because your parents or grandparents instilled it in you. This happens a lot with things like religion, politics, and the brands we purchase. If you notice, in many cases you just accepted them as the truth and did very little to research them as you matured and began to form your own opinions.

Perhaps you chose an element, such as only buying a certain brand's version of a food you like to eat. Whatever it is, play fair and get something different, something that you haven't challenged yourself with recently.

If you choose a pattern, do something like driving a different route to work, or use a different hand to brush your teeth or your hair. Get dressed in reverse by putting the opposite leg into your pants first.

You'll begin to notice that many of your daily activities, patterns, and ideas have been on automatic pilot for a while. These challenges will help you realize just how "asleep at the wheel" you've become over time, and that you can actively be more conscious and involved in the choices you're establishing or continuing.

TRANSFORMATION

- chapter two -

*Transformation — a word that instills tremendous excitement
in some and fear in others.*

You could say that transformation is a tale of two sisters — **Excitement** and **Fear**. As states of consciousness, they seem to have little in common. If you look more deeply, however, both have the power to create great turmoil and anxiety in the mind and body, and to incite tremendous emotional reactions — one positive, one negative. Each is a powerful motivating element in the dynamic law of creation that generates incredible energy within each of us.

Transformation is merely a form of alchemy, a shifting from one state to another — the morphing of **energy** and **mindset**. When we make a shift in thinking, everything within us begins to transform. Time and time again, we see that someone who was always attracted to the wrong type of person suddenly becomes a magnet once their mind has shifted, attracting that right individual who will treat them with honor, dignity, and respect. Consider the person who was raised with abuse and was in turn abusive to their loved ones. Once their mindset has been shifted, they change to become kind, generous, selfless, and thoughtful; the need for abusiveness is eliminated.

Transformation is natural and necessary to life, and yet it's the ego's greatest enemy. Transformation means change, but change means death to the fixed concepts of the ego. The ego seeks security through solid ideas, consistent patterns, and habits. It is the part of us that views our person as a separate, self-contained entity. Ego seeks control in an effort to minimize change; it does not like going in any direction other than that which is self-serving and self-gratifying.

The ego seeks to be the center of its own universe and of those around it. It is controlling — setting the stage and the characters to its liking in order to feel secure. When things don't go the way the ego desires, it reacts using anger, fear, and resentment to either lash out or adjust things to fit its comfort zone.

Fear is a component of self-preservation and employs anger and manipulative tactics like false projection to maintain control over an individual. If the individual does not buy into the false projections and insecurities staged by the ego, the ego turns on that person internally—at least until the individual realizes that they are not "one" with their ego. This is key, and usually requires a humbling experience or a conscious awareness of the ego's intent. It means that the person needs to step outside of themselves long enough to see and acknowledge what's happening.

Stepping out of this vicious cycle isn't easy because we generally identify ourselves through our egos. However, we are *not* our minds, and therefore cannot be our ego. This is a great truth that has the power to stop the ego in its tracks. In *The Power of Now*, Eckhart Tolle provides some tremendous methodologies on how to become an intense observer of the mind, which in turn can assist a person in getting a grip on the ego.

To understand ego better, it's necessary to view the components of the mind separately. First, there is the **conscious mind**. This is the part of the mind that interacts with the social and physical environments in which we live. The conscious mind is objective and has free choice over the actions of the mind and body, determining how we respond to the world surrounding us.

Second is the **ego itself.** It is the primary facilitator or operating force of the conscious mind, making it very easy to identify ourselves with the mind. Unfortunately, it conceals important elements about who we really are at our core in order to maintain control over the conscious space. To be identified with the ego is to buy into the stories and judgments that the ego feeds our conscious mind—to the point of losing our true identity. Although the ego and conscious mind may have choice—and with it, great power—the belief systems of the *critical faculty* and *subconscious* can override them completely.

The next component of the mind is the **critical faculty**, which is the barrier that maintains separation between the conscious and subconscious minds, as described in the study of hypnosis. It is derived from the beliefs that develop as the mind grows and experiences life. Think of it as a callus on a part of the foot where your shoes rub; the more rigid the critical faculty becomes, the more we lose flexibility and limit our possibilities.

The belief systems of the critical faculty filter all stimuli and input, altering them to fit its rules—the stories and judgments of the ego. It then discards the information that doesn't fit, creating our individual experience of the world. This limited experience of the world and bending of information (aka selective hearing/listening) validates our belief in the stories the ego feeds us about who we are. This helps the ego to maintain inferiority complexes, false impressions of the self, self-centeredness, and excessive self-importance manifesting as egoism, arrogance, dominance, and control. These are all tools that the ego uses for self-preservation.

Beyond the critical faculty and conscious mind is the *subjective mind*, or the **subconscious**. Unlike the conscious mind, the subconscious mind resides and vibrates at a depth beyond our ability for awareness. It is the root, thus the distinction *sub*-conscious mind. The subconscious is the origin of all thoughts and the facilitator of all creation in our lives. If you take a key and press it into soft putty, it will leave an imprint of the key. If the putty were to harden, you would have a perfect mold of the key to use for duplication purposes. Welcome to the subconscious mind!

Think about your mind as if it were a group of components used to create a mold. Whatever information penetrates through the critical faculty to the subconscious mind becomes its truth. An image of the information, feeling/emotion, or idea/thought is imprinted into it. The imprint is then stored in the critical faculty, where it becomes a fixed belief and the process of creation begins. The subconscious mind must then create what it believes to be true in order to validate its existence. It looks for any parallel it can find to align with the belief, seeking out a mental or physical connection to this alignment. The conscious mind does this first through belief, then vibration.

A human being is a complex energy system that operates at a unique rate of speed and intensity, just like sound waves are capable of vibrating across a range of frequencies. High pitches have very energetic frequencies and low pitches have slower frequencies. We've all met people who we could describe as mellow and calming or boisterous and vibrant. What we're picking up on with these individuals is their personal energy levels running at a **vibration** unique to them. An individual's energy vibrates at a level corresponding to their beliefs, attracting other energy sources of similar vibration. This is known as the **Law of Dynamic Attraction**. In this way, the subconscious creates its own customized world and expression in life.

In addition, the subconscious mind is connected to a number of higher-level energy fields, such as the spiritual or God Consciousness, cosmic consciousness, and Akashic, to name just a few. These levels of energy are said to contain all knowledge and information. Because of this connection through the subconscious mind, it is believed that human beings have access to all knowledge at all times, much like being connected to the World Wide Web. Many believe this to be the Omnipresent Mind of God, or Spirit. In fact, quantum physicists have found themselves standing on the edge of a cliff related to this topic. *The Quantum Enigma*, by Bruce Rosenblum and Fred Kuttner, elaborates on a well-know and very perplexing phenomenon one encounters at the quantum level, known quantum entanglement. In a nutshell, decades of respected scientific research implies that the universe has a fundamental consciousness.

One school of thought says that one or all of these higher levels of consciousness make up what we consider to be the mind, and that we all think and live through one single mind. In other words, the personalized expression that creates us as individuals is derived from the belief systems of the subconscious and conscious minds that filter and limit the "One Mind". If that's true, the possibility of all human expression is increased and expanded by our individual experiences.

Transformation is moving from the state of no choice or little choice to the ultimate state of power—having complete choice. Complete choice is being able to challenge your every thought and process, doing what it takes to discover their origins and the core beliefs that support them. For example, if there's a specific food someone has decided they simply don't like, they've made that distinction by choice, which is good. On the other hand, if that person doesn't like that food due to some event or programming that was imposed upon them by others (or to which they were predisposed), then by definition, they are not at choice. They have given away or had taken from them their right of choice.

In the case of my youngest son, he ceased eating all vegetables after his brother tricked him into eating a pickle he did not want to eat, saying it tasted like lettuce. The bitter flavor repulsed him so intensely that he refused to eat any vegetables from the time he was 3 or 4 years old up until the age of 14. Only then did he begin to challenge the belief system that was established by that one event; today he is eating healthier, vegetable-based foods. The result of that one action by his older brother left him a victim for at least 10 years. To his brother, it was a funny game between siblings. To his parents, it became a nightmare. Getting proper nutrition into him became much more difficult and expensive, causing us to consult a physician and purchase appropriate supplements. By being his brother's victim, he gave up all power over what he ate. He took back his power of choice by challenging his own beliefs about trying unfamiliar foods.

This may seem like a rudimentary example, but I can assure you that almost everyone makes choices based on being the victim of someone else, and we all have beliefs that go unchallenged. True transformation begins with questioning our belief system in such a way that each thing we eat, do, say, or stand up for is truly our own decision and not some conditioned response or idea transferred into us by others.

Living with dignity means being able to make independent decisions that you can stand behind, regardless of the outcome. Many people refuse to take accountability for their choices because they're afraid to be wrong. It escapes them that there is only the perception—not a judg-ment—of right or wrong.

Lack of accountability is the main reason why people get stuck. It's easier to blame others and become their victim than it is to take respon-sibility for our own actions. People are generally afraid to be incorrect or make poor decisions, but it isn't so much a matter of right or wrong choices as it is about results. If we consider the results, process them, and move forward, we'll quickly learn what works for us and what doesn't. We'll begin making better decisions for ourselves, which will achieve greater personal results. Accountability is the asphalt that paves the road to freedom, but first you have to overcome your ego and become accountable for your decisions and actions. This isn't always easy, and it usually entails a humbling experience that separates us from our ego long enough to realize that it (the ego) doesn't have the answers. This is the state of mind in which miracles happen.

Take an addict or alcoholic. Once they admit powerlessness and be-come accountable for their disease or dysfunction, they are able to step out of the trauma and struggle and are able to embrace a new level of freedom. It's a remarkable thing to watch! If you want to be released from anything in your life that you no longer want or need (such as a certain behavior pattern), then you need to embrace it. Accepting it for what it is will help you to make a new, conscious choice in the present moment.

Acceptance is vital to personal freedom. Consciousness is awareness, and it can only be found by those who are willing to see themselves honestly and realistically. The way to make this happen is to truly claim accountability. It's one thing to say the words, but it's something entirely different to say them with acceptance and understanding, acknowledg-ing that it really was you and the choices you made that created your current situation in life—even if you don't understand how it happened.

Many people look for an explanation along the lines of reincarnation or karma to accept their condition or circumstances. Instead of drawing that sort of conclusion, it's actually much easier and more effective to release blame and eliminate the ego's justifications by owning up to personal choice. **The power is in choice; choice requires awareness, and awareness requires accountability.**

Even though it's basically quite simple, it's not an easy thing to accomplish given that we live in a world where our primary obsession is to place blame on something outside ourselves. Most of the legal field is dependent on this inclination of human behavior. In fact, personal injuries have become a sort of lottery to certain people—they look for opportunities to place blame and cash in.

Let's say you're driving in a car at 90 mph on a 70 mph highway. Suddenly, there's an object or obstruction in your path such as a tire, a piece of wood or a pipe. You swerve to miss the object, hit the shoulder of the road and lose control. You flip the car five times, get out unscathed, and begin to shout obscenities. Your immediate tendency is to place blame on the person responsible for the object that you had to swerve to miss.

Not once do you give consideration to the idea that you shouldn't have been driving 90 mph in the first place. You don't think, "I screwed up. I shouldn't have been driving that fast." You know this is the truth. You know it's the core cause of your anger because you're upset with yourself, but it's easier to focus all the anger and attention on external things. By doing so, you have just given away your power. You'd rather become the poor victim of the person that is responsible for the debris. He gets the blame and you get the really cool victim story to tell your friends. Of course, everyone you tell your story to isn't stupid, and they walk away thinking, "What an idiot, it would have never happened if he wasn't driving so fast. Good thing he didn't hit someone, or have his children in the car. He deserved that ticket." You can be certain that the ones who aren't saying that are thinking it, and they're just grateful it didn't happen to them.

Honestly, who wants to be thought of as a powerless victim in life? I certainly don't! I want power. I want to feel good about my life experience. Sure, I screw up all the time, but having the integrity to stand up and admit that it was a choice I made grants me esteem in my community, gives me dignity, and wins me great respect. It grants me power in life—my own life.

I am not seeking control, and this shouldn't be confused with control. People who are control freaks are suffering from the same affliction, but in a different way. They're going to make sure they are nobody's victim by controlling every possible detail—to the point of driving everyone around them crazy. They never allow things to just happen, and will force a square peg into a round hole if they have to. If one day they find one that doesn't fit or can't be forced, they'll blame you or someone else because they believe they can do no wrong. This personality can be as bad as the perpetual victim, and yet it's no guarantee that they aren't victims themselves, only cloaked in a different cape.

The only real power you have in life is your ability to be at choice in every aspect of your life. The more conscious you become of the various domains you participate in, the more you'll be at choice.

Conscious awareness is a tremendous product of accountability and responsibility. The more willing you are to be honest with yourself concerning who you really are and the choices you've made, the greater your capacity for accountability. This results in a higher conscious awareness and realization of self. The higher your conscious awareness, the greater your capacity for making independent choices (choices free from prior programming) in all aspects of your life. This defines you as a person of great personal power.

The really successful people throughout time have had a few things in common—they were people of high conscious awareness, impeccable accountability, and they were not afraid to be wrong. They are the people who could make a choice and stand behind it, no matter what the outcome might be.

A person who has freed their mind has less static bogging down their interactions in the world. The energy that they emit from their thoughts becomes healthier, essentially vibrating with greater ease and purity—they have discovered how to find their Flow. Freeing themselves from disrupting, negative thoughts brings back their excitement for life and its possibilities, creating a cleaner center of attraction.

Fear is defensive; it feeds off of negativity and protects itself by pushing things away—even good things. Cleaning up the distortion in your thought processes frees the mind by using choice to override the fears caused by the ego's stories. Addressing and removing the fears counteracts the energy that pushes things away from you, meaning that you become more open to the world. The result of that is what many refer to as the Law of Attraction. Removing or lowering those walls of resistance allows positive, desirable solutions into your life.

EXERCISE AWARENESS

I invite you to find a quiet place where you cannot be disturbed, and then allow yourself to sit quietly for about 20 to 30 minutes. Only listen.

You'll quickly notice that life around you is not so quiet.

First, you'll have to contend with the sounds in your head and the little voice that will start to run amuck. Second, begin to notice that even in silence there are numerous sounds around you all the time. Third, you'll probably realize just how hard it is to focus your mind without intrusions from internal and external noise.

More than likely, you'll probably find that this process is much harder than you had anticipated, primarily because of the noise in your own head. If you keep going, however, your awareness of the noise in and around you will begin to heighten.

Now focus your eyes on a specific object or point in the room. Hold that gaze and begin to rub your thumb and index finger together, concentrating on that sensation while holding your gaze. Noise may begin to quiet as your attention increasingly focuses on your fingers. This is awareness, and awareness is key to any transformational experience.

VALIDATION OF THE SELF

- chapter three -

As you believe, so shall it be.

We've all heard that if you believe you can do something, you can, but if you don't believe you can do it, you're defeated before you begin. Your belief system controls the experience that you'll have in this life, and there's no greater physical truth than that. As you believe, so it is.

How can a simple belief control your entire life experience?

As a personal coach working in the self-development field, it's been truly astonishing to me how quickly simple principles can work to impact and empower individuals toward tremendous transformation. It's been amazing to observe people as they apply the formulas and principles that I share with them, and to see them go on to live with greater joy, excitement, and freedom.

As wonderful as those situations have been, some have come to me for assistance achieving a breakthrough in their life but have needed something beyond my capabilities. They had experiences that were too traumatic for them to think about, much less discuss—usually violence, rape, or similar events. Due to the fact that the coaching I do is primarily centered on linguistics (encompassing our internal dialogue, for the most part) these individuals were out of my reach. They had a barrier hindering discussion about these events, preventing me from being able to get in and help them work through it. We tried numerous techniques, but simply didn't make much progress.

At one point, there were several people who were all struggling with this. I desperately wanted to help them, so I began to meditate and reflect on what I could do differently or do more of in order to reach those breakthroughs. It was just unacceptable that the medical and psychology fields had failed them, and now I was failing them, too.

How I could not reach these individuals that were so obviously suffering? The predicament had me baffled, and I wanted to help. I knew we needed to get past their conscious objections, but how? One day, it hit me. I thought about how I had bypassed my own consciousness to manage pain issues using self-hypnosis techniques. In that moment, I knew that I needed to go to school for hypnosis. Because I didn't know exactly where to start, I trusted the Universe to guide me, and it did.

In those days, I was doing some coaching at a little New Age complex in Baton Rouge, and would utilize a biofeedback device as an aid during the sessions. It was a very powerful tool, and I had recorded videos for my clients to take home that illustrated their energy patterns while I was coaching them. After hearing about the videos, a gentleman walked up and asked if I might be interested in doing some video work for his school, possibly as a trade. I explained that I would be happy to discuss it with him, and that I had a camera and the necessary equipment. I then asked him what type of school he was referring to, and wouldn't you know, he owned a school for hypnosis. *Bingo!*

Armed with a certification in hypnotherapy, I was finally content that I had the necessary tools and understanding to make a difference for nearly anyone needing help, as long as they truly wanted to be helped. My ability to coach had grown with my newfound knowledge of how the subconscious mind and conscious mind worked together. I had at last confirmed a longtime suspicion—*our beliefs control our experience and outcomes in life.*

When we come into the world, we're a blank canvas, with our conscious mind and subconscious mind fully intact. We're ready to gather experiences, to develop and mold this thing we call our life—our **self**. If you were to draw a target consisting of three concentric circles, with the center being the subconscious mind, the outer ring being the conscious mind, and the middle ring (the critical faculty) acting as a barrier between them, then you would have a clear illustration of how they relate to one another.

When we absorb new information, it imprints into the subconscious mind and we begin to develop a belief based on the imprint. Bear in mind that the subconscious is subjective; it needs the critical faculty to protect it by filtering the incoming data properly. Without a filter, it would be inundated by a tremendous amount of conflicting information coming in from the environment, which would stifle us to the point that we couldn't function.

The conscious and subconscious minds formulate beliefs in different ways. If we're told the stove is hot, then we have a *belief* that the stove is hot. We are making an assumption based on information provided to us that we choose to accept as true. However, if we touch that stove to test it for ourselves, we now *know* it's hot, and we form accompanying judgments regarding hot stoves. Let me give you a clearer illustration about how it affects us.

Let's say that there are two people, and that one has been taught that the absence of color is black, whereas the other was taught that the absence of color is white. The two would look at the same thing and have a completely different belief as to what it is. They could argue forever, never reaching any conclusion except that the other was wrong. So what is the truth? The truth is, they are both absolutely correct *based on their belief system*. The truth—and what we consider right or wrong—are all based on what our present belief system holds as true. For those two individuals, the subconscious mind has been imprinted with their beliefs, and that information is now a conscious part of who they are. Their beliefs about the absence of color are firmly implanted into the critical faculty.

The critical faculty's primary job is to prevent contradictory thoughts from entering and collapsing either its own structure or that of the subconscious mind. The conscious mind then creates a system of judgments and reasoning/stories to validate and protect the belief, regardless of external standpoints for that belief. If the belief and its corresponding judgments become jeopardized, then the fear-based ego jumps in to defend and rationalize it.

If you're still with me on this, then you're on track towards truly grasping many of the habits, patterns, and thought processes that plague us as humans. This topic may be a little complex, but don't feel concerned if you don't get it right away! As you continue through the text, upcoming topics will help you to understand it a little bit at a time.

Let's look at it again. The subconscious mind becomes imprinted with information from which it creates a belief. The belief is then stored in a protective barrier of the mind called the critical faculty, which in turn protects the subjective mind from any new information that is contrary to that belief. To accomplish this, the conscious mind creates a set of judgments about the world at large, based on the belief. The ego then protects these judgments and beliefs, typically through fear-based responses. Finally, the ego builds a story around the belief and its accompanying judgments, becoming a fortress to stand behind as it defends the belief system.

Imagine you're building a house of cards or a tower of blocks. There are no beams or support columns to hold up the walls and roof; the construction itself acts as both the foundation and structure. This is sort of how the mind is put together, with structure and foundation as one. The ego is in a constant state of vigilance to ensure that no single block or card will fall, something that would cause a collapse to the rest of the structure. This is extremely important to the fragile ego, because its very existence is based on these beliefs and the supporting stories that hold them up.

Note: I should mention that this does not always apply to things that have been learned in a traditional cognitive manner (such as reading, math, or job skills) because the proper supporting elements have been put in place through the learning process.

We have all heard of, and quite probably experienced, buyer's remorse, otherwise known as **cognitive dissonance**. This is when we buy something (usually a big-ticket item), thinking we're making a good purchasing decision and perhaps a very unique selection. Almost invariably, we immediately begin to question our actions and in some cases, regret begins to set in. We then leave the store, only to suddenly notice that the same product is everywhere. We just haven't been aware of it before, so to speak. This frequently happens when you drive a car off of the dealership lot. Suddenly, the whole world seems to be driving the same car as you! You now have a sense of making a good purchase decision because many other people have chosen the same car. This is known as **validation**, and is a very important process in pacifying our security instinct. With a car purchase, the process is usually more extreme, but most of us have had this experience in one form or another.

Now imagine that you've bought into a set of beliefs in your life. Through your acquired belief system, you seek every possible validation for who you have become. This has its pros and cons. It does serve to make us feel better about ourselves, but it's a function of fear and insecurity—more of a linguistic fear than a biological fear, but a fear nonetheless. Having the roots of our security based in fear is almost never a good thing, and is normally considered dysfunctional.

You may have been raised in a dysfunctional family, and from a very young age observed verbal abuse, neglect, and in some cases, physical and sexual abuse. The beliefs that were imprinted in you were defining interpersonal family relationships, worthless feelings about yourself, and a sense of not being lovable. You grow up, and perhaps get married or enter into a long-term relationship, but suddenly you find yourself in a victim/perpetrator exchange with the man or woman that you love. Nothing you do is ever good enough, and there's neglect and assorted abuses. You just don't understand how you could have picked the wrong spouse, but you're certain they're to blame for misleading you about themselves. You're in a dilemma, but you break out of that relationship after a number of years have passed. You feel like you've wasted so much time and need to move on with your life. Eventually, you start to date again and meet someone you really like being around. The two of you seem to be a great match and you move in together, but soon the world begins to fall apart and you get hurt by some action of theirs. You still don't see your role in it, even though you're quite sure you have some small part. You're positive that they really are to blame for things not working out. You break up and wonder, "How I could have been attracted to the wrong person again? What's wrong with me?" The key word here is ME.

The truth is there is nothing *wrong* with you. You're functioning according to design. You're going out in life and validating who and what you are based on the beliefs that were instilled in you as a child. The ego/self, critical faculty, and subconscious are working in unison to bring you the experience that you need—based on your beliefs—so that you're able to validate your existence. If you're thinking that this sounds messed up, you're absolutely right!

Over and over, we slip into the same patterns in different guises, creating the same self-defeating situations until something so horrible happens that it destroys our mechanism and allows new information to penetrate the system.

The critical faculty needs to be penetrated deeply enough to break down the system completely and allow new information to come through. This is the beginning of restaging our mindset. Once this occurs, seemingly hopeless situations begin to have new options and greater possibilities. The door to freedom has been cracked open, humility has entered, and transformation can begin. A good coach would jump in at this point and kick the door wide open, so that you can't shut it again unconsciously. A light begins to shine into the dark areas of the mind and you begin to see yourself—your true self. You become awakened.

The validation process of the mind is very important to our level of personal security. Confidence requires a certain sense of security, and we must have confidence in certain areas in order to live. Insecurity is a function of the fear-based ego. What if none of us had any confidence or security in our ability to drive? Could you imagine what the roads might look like? What if we didn't trust anyone else to prepare our food? Do you think there would be restaurants? Or how about doctors and medical professionals? There wouldn't be any, because we would be too afraid to use them. Our choice would be to choose which we're more afraid of—the doctor or the illness—and act accordingly.

We need to have the confidence that arises from the validation process. As I see it, the problem is that we get so wrapped up in ourselves that we lose track of the things for which we're seeking validation. We start looking for validation of the very things we *don't* want in our lives, instead of what we do want, such as financial failures instead of successes, proof that relationships don't work instead of proof that they do, and evidence of our worthlessness instead of value and personal success. Are we attracting these negative experiences to us like a magnet, or are we just creating them from what life provides to us? Regardless of the underlying dynamics, how can we change this? The answer is simple, but not as easy to see, which is where having a coach, counselor or some good, honest friends and a support system comes into play. It's also where doing self-development workshops, seminars, retreats, and other activities of that nature can be useful. We all need someone to see us as who we are and to be honest with us. This is a crucial step to maintaining balance, at least until we're capable of guiding and observing ourselves. Even upon reaching this stage, a good coach or support system can be invaluable in helping us maintain an honest point of self-observation.

EXERCISE SELF-ASSESSMENT

On a sheet of paper, write down 10 beliefs or thought patterns that you tend to focus on frequently—20 if you're really bold. Attempt to make them some of your more common internal dialogues. Now be honest about the way you see yourself. In a column next to each thought, write down whether it is a positive or negative viewpoint and whether it is based in fear or based in security.

By doing this exercise, you will have a more comprehensive idea of how you look at life. Next, simply take each statement that is based in fear and write a short, but honest evaluation as to why you see it (or yourself) the way that you do. Skip a line and write down how you can shift that belief or thought pattern to be grounded more in confidence and security. If you draw a blank while thinking about how you can shift the belief, simply rewrite the thought pattern or belief statement again, but in a positive framework centered in security and confidence.

THE STORY

- chapter four -

As the World Turns, so do the Days of Our Lives

Like any good soap opera, a story has to be compelling—having a number of good plots and consistent underlying themes. When it comes to internal stories, the theme never really changes; despite a wide variety of story lines, the underlying theme is victimization, or in some rare cases, perpetration.

That's right, the primary idea behind nearly all stories is to illustrate how we have become someone's victim—how we have been wronged and how our life has not worked out because of someone else's actions or wrongdoing or how we didn't get a fair shot. This could be a person or an institution, or sometimes just "the fate of the gods," but the central idea is that I did nothing wrong and *I was wronged and have good reason to be indignant and upset, even vengeful, because of it.* Don't believe me? Go read about a few divorce cases—people who initially thought the world of each other now blame the other person for their entire life not being "right."

These are the days of our lives, no pun intended. Our stories have a purpose much more significant than being a victim; they're also mechanisms that guard against anyone penetrating the critical faculty. Recall that the ego is vigilantly using the critical faculty and objective mind to protect its belief systems. If any one of them are penetrated and destroyed, then that aspect of the ego is destroyed. Think about it—if the primary instinctual mindset of any animal or human being is preservation of life, then the ego will likewise do whatever it can to prevent what it believes to be death to any part of itself. In other words, the system will do whatever is necessary to preserve what it believes to be the truth, even if it's the very thing destroying the system.

Consider that for a minute. Unless we're programmed for success in life from the outset and protected from any programming to the contrary, at some point, we'll have to confront change, as well as our programming, or be victims of it. In actuality, change is the one thing in life that is consistent and can be absolutely counted on. But even though it may be a dominant aspect of living, the ego sees change as a killing off of the known and a venture into the unknown. It interprets itself as dying, and fights to survive by using a linguistic-based fear. The ego fears the unknown and takes security in the known. This is the great internal struggle of human beings; it is not man against man, but man against himself. By working these things out within ourselves, we would have no reason for war or fighting of any kind; we would be pliable—able to shift and change with the times. We would be open-minded and unbothered by compromise, and we would be capable of making all the necessary changes to save our environment quickly and without pain.

The pain that we experience is in exact proportion to our resistance to change.

In one of her songs, the artist Jewel once wrote, "Nature has a way of breaking that which does not bend." All too often, we're so embedded in our stories and the protection they provide that nature has to break us. We cling to the security they offer, only to become inflexible. The more set we become in the story, the stronger the blow life has to hand out to teach us change and flexibility. It's the stories that we stand behind with extreme conviction that evolve into barricades, holding anything at bay that could cause change and subsequently push us into the unknown. We also become self-righteous and indignant if anyone gets close to violating the space around our stories. Have you ever stopped for a moment in the middle of an argument or debate, or while defending some hard-set principle or idea, and asked yourself what it is you're defending? You might be surprised to discover that you can peel back your answers like the layers of an onion. As you strip away each layer, you'll notice that you're defending some set of judgments based on a belief system you have. Your reaction, or defense, is nothing more than the fear of having your belief system penetrated, making you wrong about something you hold as a personal truth. This is really the basis for all argument.

Have you ever heard the statement, "Would you rather be happy or right?" If you've had it posed to you while you were deeply engaged in making a point, it seems incredibly messed up—absolutely on the money, but messed up, nonetheless. I always felt like it was an instant loss of the point to just give up the argument, simply because I didn't get to win. But truthfully, that's a choice we have—would we rather be right than happy? If *right* is your answer, then you may want to look at *why*—what are you protecting, what's your motive, and what exactly are you trying to prove to yourself? If your answer is *happy*, then the point should no longer matter, but as we all know, for most of us it does.

I wasn't able to figure out why I just couldn't be right *and* happy, and eventually, I discovered that I could. The fact is that what I hold as truth is right for me—just not necessarily anyone else, and I really don't need to defend that. What is right for you and what is right for me are not the same. No matter how similar they may appear, they will never match up with perfect accuracy because perspective is filtered through our environmental input and experience of life. Therefore, no two perspectives or points can ever be exactly the same. In short, what is right for you has to be right, and what is right for me, although different from you, is right, as well. As I stated earlier, right and wrong are only based on our perspective at that moment.

Let's look back at the concept of stories. Our stories, along with all they defend, are right for each of us as individuals, regardless of what others think. Our reality is based on perception, and we create our lives through that perception. If this is the case, aren't we only hurting ourselves by sticking to our stories? Aren't our stories filtering our perception of the world and therefore serving up all present and future experiences based on those mindsets?

In a nutshell, *we continue to find validation for our belief systems*. The ego creates stories to protect the belief systems and all of their judgments, while the protection mechanism operates to attract more validating experiences to support those systems. We're creating our reality based on our past experiences of being a victim.

Here is an example of the power of belief. Have you ever had someone tell you terrible things about a person before you met them? You know, "That Mary Jo woman is a bitch," or something similar. Immediately upon meeting Mary Jo, all you can see and hear is how much of a bitch she is, just the way your friend described. Or, you decide to try something new, like yoga, for instance, only to have someone tell you about their own negative personal experience with that activity. Because of that, when you're there, you notice a similar experience is evolving. Basically, they have stolen your experience by influencing you with their judgments and beliefs ahead of time, instead of letting you have your own. In spite of this, you may have noticed that by simply putting what they said out of your mind that your experience is distinctly different from theirs. Mary Jo is actually a pretty cool lady, or the experience with your new adventure is really quite nice. The power of suggestion is a very strong influencer when it comes to our experiences. We are capable of bending any event, situation and condition to our preconceived beliefs or opinions about it.

At one point in my life, I was injured severely and had to walk with a cane. It was a very depressing time for me, and I thought I would never fully regain my balance and be able to walk normally. To top it all off, people were constantly talking about my situation and criticizing. They questioned the severity of my injuries because I was engaged in a third-party legal action regarding negligence on the part of the company involved. I was very self-conscious and greatly disturbed by their responses. On the one hand, it made me feel stripped of power to walk with a cane, but on the other, I felt like it was better then falling and hurting myself even worse. It put me in a difficult situation; I didn't like the negative reactions or the disempowering feeling.

After walking with this cane for five years, I finally let go and made the decision to live without it. A year later, still with a severe limp, I went to a seminar and learned about **mechanisms**, which are mindsets we have that twist and mold things to our desired effect or belief, and how they affect us and the people around us. What I learned was that I had a conversation in my head (about what people with my degree of injuries and in my condition should look like) and I couldn't break out of that image. I felt small because I now needed assistance, and I was very judgmental of my circumstances and of myself. But then I had a moment of clarity. I realized I had actually created myself in the image of my beliefs regarding people with similar injuries. When I realized this, it was electric. Within a couple of hours, someone noticed that I had completely stopped limping.

It was like a miracle had happened, but the truth was that I had actually taken complete ownership for my part in the accident and for my condition, and immediately became aware of how my beliefs and stories dealing with that accident and litigation had held me prisoner. It didn't stop the pain, but the pain didn't have to bear evidence for the world to see any longer.

When I later analyzed what happened, I realized that my story and the belief system regarding this area of my life had been penetrated. I released the victim story in that moment, and my body immediately adjusted to it. To date, it's still one of the most powerful experiences in my life; it was like a miracle healing, except that I was behind the curtain and saw the wizard. To this day, I might occasionally show a little favor toward one side, but no one can tell when they meet me that I have or have ever had a problem of that nature, much less to that extent. I refuse to buy back into those beliefs, and I truly believe that is what makes the difference.

The stories that we live in shape our lives, supporting us as we create new opportunities to validate our victim stories and beliefs. It is these stories that work to perpetuate a state of rigidity in the name of security and fear of the unknown. In turn, this rigidity is the mindset that ultimately lands us on the rocks, because "nature has a way of breaking that which does not bend." Change really is growth, and growth is the law of life.

EXERCISE STORIES

With pen and paper, make a list of the stories in your life that you defend. The story of why you look the way you do, act the way you do, live the way you do or have the job you have. Not all stories are negative. What is the story behind not buying the car you want, the boat you want or having the business or job you want? What is the story behind why your relationship isn't the best it could be or your children aren't the way you would like them to be? What is your family story or your in-law story or what about the last bad breakup? Go over these explanations and decide if they make you feel empowered or disempowered. Discover the thoughts within these stories that make you feel good or bad, and why. These are important things to know. Now reframe and change them to a more desired outcome. You will be amazed at how your life will change when you embody these new views of the same old stories.

AWARENESS

- chapter five -

Penetration, Deflation, and Separation are the only path
to real observation of truth.

As a man thinketh, so it is. I've read numerous variations on this statement over the years, and have seen it proven time and time again in my
own life and in the lives of my clients. It takes great courage to go against
all you know to be true, break out of lifelong patterns, and embrace
change. It means going up against what you see as your *self.*

Awareness is the only way out of the chains that bind us to our
stories, and it doesn't matter whether they're about victimhood, perpetration, fantasy, or any number of other personal plots. They prevent us
from maintaining balance in our lives and they hold us back, keeping
us from realizing our greatest potential in life—finding our true selves.
Awareness is our light at the end of the tunnel.

Before we can begin to shift and change what is,
we must first have awareness of what isn't.

Before we can take ownership for our lives,
we must first be aware that we don't own our lives.

Before we can know,
we must first be aware that we don't know,
and may never truly know.

Before we can truly live in choice,
we must first be aware that a greater possibility
for choice exists.

To make a shift takes great conscious effort, but once we do it, change
begins to come naturally and will continue if we're vigilant. We are not
one-dimensional beings; awareness is not an event that takes place on

merely one level of our lives. Each of us is richly layered with **conversations** that make up our entire mental, physical, and emotional being. As we become awakened at one level, we begin to notice new possibilities at another. Awakening is a continuous process, like the gradual unfolding of a rosebud into a lush, mature bloom. The outer layers must release before the deeper layers can loosen and open, and it happens one petal, one layer, at a time. The more we begin to encourage conscious observance of ourselves, the greater our awareness of who we are, what we are, and how we relate to the world.

Awareness is an **unfoldment** of that which is within and around us—a heightened consciousness of both our internal and external environments. As it unfolds, we begin to shift, creating an entirely different vantage point in our lives. From that point we make new **distinctions**. These distinctions allow us to see, hear, and feel the world in a way we haven't previously experienced.

To understand unfoldment, you first have to accept that we are linguistic beings—that our human experience is heavily immersed in communication and language. We even have conversations with ourselves! We use language to assist us in making sense of the world from our unique perspective, but those dialogues don't just vanish, especially if we need to use them repeatedly. They go on to become the underlying structure that dictates what we do, think and desire, sort of like a dictionary we keep for reference purposes to help us process new material.

These layers of words and phrases define our perception and accumulate until they're stacked so high and are layered so densely that you can no longer see the individual dialogues that guide your everyday choices. You use these embedded conversations as justifications and rationalizations for the way you are and the way you live. They become your truth. Peeling back the layers of these dialogues shifts you out of your default viewpoint. This immediately—almost electrically—changes your perception of the world and how you define and create your life. Ultimately, the old dialogues are replaced by these new conversations stemming from awareness.

Based on this information, it is safe to say that our linguistic make-up dictates our experience in life in a couple of ways. First, it filters the information coming in based on our perception of the truth. Second, it determines our view of the world and how we experience it. It may seem a little hocus-pocus at first, but it is solid science. Everything we experience in life is perceived by our ability to process it in speech. Therefore, if both our internal and external dialogues are focused a certain way, we will get a very specific result.

Suppose you're in a new relationship, and everything is so rosy that all you see is your partner's good attributes. The more good you observe and acknowledge (specific focus), the more good you'll discover, almost like a never-ending stream of goodness. Then, as time passes and the new car smell fades, you may begin noticing habits and patterns that you didn't recognize before. You may not be too thrilled about some of them (the focus is shifting). Nevertheless, those good memories from before are still acting to whitewash the negative.

Inevitably, you start to see more and more of those little things and you begin to watch for them, all because focus has shifted to a specific direction. You pay such close attention that it's as if your partner is riddled with traits that just annoy you or that you find unacceptable. Even though you try pointing them out, it just continues. Maybe your partner will suppress some of them for a moment, but you find that they pop up someplace else. It's as if your awareness of them can't be turned off (and it can't until you once again shift your focus)! The more you look at them, the more they begin to show themselves. Soon, you can't stand it and you break up.

What really happened here? Did we create this dilemma by concentrating on it or did it simply unfold? Actually, it's a bit of both. In meditation, when you focus your mind on a given subject (set your inner dialogue to neutral or in a focused direction) the mind naturally unfolds and expands in that direction. So, when you focused on the good things, they kept unfolding as your awareness of them expanded, but when you turned it toward the negative, the same process happened, but your awareness unfolded in a negative direction. We're always in an expanding awareness through our internal dialogues. The objective is to *purposely* focus your awareness and its unfoldment in a direction of your desired outcome.

During one particular relationship, I started to experience this very common occurrence for myself. I decided to do an experiment. Every day, I would wake up and focus my inner dialogue on being grateful for all the wonderful attributes of my partner. I consciously decided that I would choose to see only her goodness, as I had done so many times with the people I coach. I would only think positive thoughts where she was concerned and cast out any thoughts to the contrary. The results were staggering, like a cascading waterfall. It wasn't that I didn't see some things that were unappealing to me, but the rush of wonderful attributes overshadowed anything else I witnessed. It was incredible. Like Alan Cohen says, "The better it gets, the better it gets." It was truly an amazing experience. The more aware I became of how extraordinary she was, the more beauty, goodness, and wonderment unfolded.

So, how do we build awareness and focus it?

Awareness is a state of being conscious or awake to everything going on around us. It's a mindset that allows us to see and hear things the way they are, not as an interpretation based on our experiences, programming, judgments, and beliefs. It is being aware of ourselves, our tendencies, our personal judgments, and our belief systems in order to **separate** and set them aside so that we may be at greater choice without their influence. As we separate ourselves from automatic thinking by becoming a conscious observer, we begin to see new choices we didn't see before.

Filtering is one of the largest contributors to people falling into somnambulism (a waking sleep). As their personal beliefs and judgments develop and the layers become thicker, people become more rigid and certain that they KNOW. This can quickly turn into arrogance, excessive confidence, or a certainty that they're right about virtually everything and that everyone else is wrong. They leave little room in their beliefs for error or compromise, and are convinced that the world is exactly as they see it. The truth is that the world *is* exactly as they see it—for them, just not anyone else. In an unaware state, each of us only sees the world as we filter it.

Our filtering system is the little voice in our head. If you're asking yourself, "What little voice?" . . . that's the one! To illustrate this a little better, start out by considering this: when we're listening to others, we're only hearing about one in five words (according to some ontological breakdowns of the communications model). The rest of the time, we're "listening" to *ourselves*—either what we're planning to say next, or reinterpreting what we're currently being told (filtering) to fit our knowledge base. Go ahead and try observing this in your next conversation with someone. Even at a ratio of one out of five words, we hear and listen pretty well. You see, the actual process of listening is more than just hearing words—it is truly grasping what the other person is communicating, and not your interpretation of what they're saying.

It's important to understand that listening is a process that goes beyond the ears, and is actually a complete biological experience—we listen with our entire being. When we listen with our entire being, we receive the message **energetically**. We sense the entirety of what is being presented—the words we hear, the body language we see, tone and intonations of the voice, and the subtext to the conversation—as a result of that person's internal dialogue and of course, their true intent. This is true listening.

When listening to someone from simply an auditory standpoint, your internal voice filters the information based on what you already know and accept as truth—your personal beliefs and subsequent judgments. For instance, if it were your opinion that the world is flat, and some-one is explaining a concept that was based on the world being round, your mind would twist what you hear in order to provide you with an interpretation based on the world being flat, *because that is what you know* (knowledge base) *and believe to be true.*

This is well supported by many explanations of the cognitive process of learning. At least one explanation of the building blocks of learning takes into consideration that at any time, an individual must possess 75 percent previously known and accepted information and only 25 percent new information to create the **connective tissue** needed for learning take place. What this simply means is that without a frame of known refer-ence, it is very difficult for us to retain new information and learn.

Think back to your time in school, and how the teachers spent time reinforcing what you learned the year before, prior to presenting new material. They were establishing the connective tissue for attaching the new information. As you got older and progressed through the grade levels, they spent less time on review (strengthening connective tissue) and more time giving you new information because they assumed your previous knowledge was strongly in place.

In my coaching, I refer to this as **templating** (a form of relativism). If the mind is unable to adapt (template) the information in a way that ad-heres to the belief systems already in place, it will usually label the new information as wrong, discard it, and resort back to the mindset that its original stance is correct. This is a form of selective hearing, filtering out that which doesn't fit or can't be reinterpreted according to current belief systems. As we stated earlier, "As you believe, so it is," and this is part of that concept. In other words, whatever your belief system, not only do you keep telling yourself the same things and looking for validation of them, you also filter content and experiences *based* on your belief sys-tems, persistently making you right in your world and expanding your awareness in a very controlled direction. This process becomes a vicious cycle that is extraordinarily difficult to break.

When I was younger, I was a very selfish individual. I had even been told this as a small child. There was an underlying motive to everything that I did, the objective being to get my own way. I was so focused on what I was trying to achieve for myself that I was oblivious to the effect on those around me. I stepped on people many times, unaware of what I was doing. I never got it. You see, I didn't think I was selfish. I would look at the things I thought were good about me, such as being sensitive and generous. I would go out of my way to help others and do things for people, even giving thoughtful gifts to those I loved. The entire time, though, I was actually focused on what I was getting back. It took many years to see this about myself.

When I finally realized my selfish programming, I began to see that even my giving and doing for others was actually out of self-centeredness. It was so that I could get what I wanted or so others would owe me. Sometimes, I just wanted the recognition to make me feel better about myself. You might ask, "What's wrong with that?" but I assure you, it is selfish and self-centered because the focus was on myself and not the other party. Don't get me wrong, I'm not saying that it's a reason to stop doing good things for others, but it is self-centered.

When it finally dawned on me how self-absorbed I really was, I began to see how my mind had twisted everything into an interpretation that convinced me I was good and generous. I realized that not only had I manipulated others, I was manipulating myself as well—flattering myself with a falsely inflated idea of who I was. Grandiosity was alive and well, and my ego made sure it stayed that way until life handed me circumstances that brought me a greater awareness.

We often have behavioral patterns of which we're completely oblivious. Many of them show up in our ability to communicate with others, and are a very easy way to observe the lack of awareness that we have in our lives. Have you ever been with someone who habitually interrupts, and yet they'll stand there and deny it, or complain about other people who do the same thing? How about someone who is constantly demeaning, or feels the need to one-up everyone during a conversation? These are common blind spots that conceal larger issues and deal with a lack of awareness. Most of these people are not at choice. They have developed a pattern, are completely unaware of it, and will look the other way if it ever becomes evident. Many of our patterns are unconscious and go unchecked, which means we have given up the power of choice in how we communicate, based on our lack of awareness.

To bring the mind to a new state of awareness, there must be a **penetration** of the ego. We penetrate the ego by shining a light into the dark region of our unchallenged belief systems, stories, and judgments—the very things that we have accepted to be absolute and true in our lives. By challenging these absolutes, we may begin to realize that they're no longer true and perhaps never were. This works to **deflate** the ego's defense mechanisms in order to create a **separation** between the observer (oneself) and the observed. The observer is the "self" with heightened consciousness—the awareness of self. The observed is the "program" part of our make-up—our habits and patterns. Essentially, we become neutral spectators of ourselves and our habits, patterns, stories, and judgments. In this way, we can then stall and disarm the **thrownness** of our patterns and belief systems, opening the door to a new world of possibilities.

A very close friend of mine wasn't very interested in the field of self-development, or so I thought. One day, she began telling me about an experience she had learning a form of meditation, one of many things she had started trying out. The conversation was going well until I began sharing some of my own experiences with meditation. I noticed her body shift, and inquired as to what was wrong. She informed me that every time she tried to learn about something new in an area familiar to me, I would steal her feelings of specialness for it by sharing stories of my own and of what she could expect in the future. She was a beginner, and the experiences she was having were as special to her in that moment as mine had been to me. She didn't need to hear what she had to look forward to, or have her excitement diminished by stories from someone farther along the path. She was great right where she was, and simply needed acknowledgement.

Because I cared for her so much, her admission immediately *penetrated* and *deflated* my ego so substantially that it woke me up, and I became aware that I was diminishing her unintentionally and supporting her very ineffectively. She later explained that this was why she hadn't pursued much in the field of self-development. Becoming aware of my tendencies and patterns *separated* me from my thrownness in this area, and brought me greater choice in how I wanted to support her and communicate with her in the future. I embraced her present state as a beginner, and it was very rewarding to experience it through her eyes.

When we become aware of who and what we are, and more importantly, where we are in life, it makes it easier to move forward. It is unnecessary to relive a situation, condition, or circumstance to overcome it—simply acknowledging the current discourse and/or mindset is enough. For example, have you ever called someone for directions when you were really lost, but couldn't explain to them where you were? No matter how well you know where you're going, the details of your current location have a significant impact on how you proceed. That's where awareness comes in. By gaining a sliver of self-awareness, you will discover that you have a point of reference to begin your journey toward enlightenment, deeper awareness, and greater choice in life.

From that point, we can evolve our awareness in a focused manner, choosing to first go within and learn about ourselves and the things that motivate and drive us. By doing this, we begin to see the world as it is, and not as we create it unconsciously in our minds. Penetration of the ego, its conversations, and our belief systems allows us to achieve separation by creating greater consciousness. Things become very obvious. It seems that everything and everyone changes, but actually, we're the ones who have changed, simply by shifting our awareness. This is the starting point for developing a clear point of attraction.

EXERCISE AWARENESS

Quiet your mind for a moment and see if you can observe yourself from outside of your body. At first this can be very difficult, so for now, just start using your imagination. Imagine yourself outside of your body, as if you are observing it from some outer perspective of your choice. Pay attention to all of the details you can bring forth, noticing how you see yourself. Take a moment to reflect back to situations and circumstances in your life when you were around others. Now, concentrate and focus very intently on this observation as if you were a neutral third person doing this. How do you see yourself? Do you look as you see yourself in a mirror? Do you see yourself the way you think others see you or the way *you* see you? Can you see the good traits that others appreciate about you, or just the criticisms that you make about yourself? Can you truly see your goodness, the very extraordinary phenomenon that you are? Do you see the shortcomings that others see in you? Do you notice how you act and communicate in social situations? Can you see how you show up as a friend and supporter to the people around you? Is there anything else that you're noticing?

Now think about these questions and go through them. I strongly suggest that you right them down. A proper, written observation of yourself can be very powerful.

BONUS EXERCISE

Note: Do this exercise only if you feel you can handle it.

After you have done this exercise and neutrally observed yourself while reflecting back on situations and circumstances in your life, ask a good friend if they could give you an honest observation of how you are, publicly and privately. Next, compare notes to see how accurate your observations were. This can be very powerful and enlightening after you have made your assessments.

THOUGHTS

- chapter six -

As a man thinks, so goes his heart and soul.

Each day, thoughts stream recklessly through our minds by the thousands. Most of them receive no attention, while others we merely observe with great curiosity and wonder. Some thoughts, however, force us to pause for further investigation, perhaps even dwell upon them. Though most people would say there's no harm to that, the thoughts we entertain will go on to become thought patterns, and those patterns begin to embed themselves as beliefs or supporting stories. The next thing you know, the subconscious is attracting them into our lives, staging our internal environment and everything around us to align with those thought patterns.

At this point, I'd like to make a critical distinction. **Thoughts** are merely the random things that pass through the mind. **Thinking** is a process of dialogue, whether you're having a conversation with yourself or with someone else. A process requires some kind of focus and effort in order to occur.

The thoughts that fly through your head all day have no power over you; they simply come and go. It's almost like scrolling through radio stations until one sounds interesting enough that you tune in. It's once you "tune in" that you start to *think* about that thought. As I'm writing this book, thoughts have been rushing through my head, but only those that I feel deeply about will stir me to action. The rest of that stream of consciousness is released to simply run in the background.

In the same way that I select thoughts and expand upon them by writing them down, the subconscious also "writes down" each thought that you entertain for any length of time. The more you start to entertain certain thoughts as a habit, the more deeply their pattern sets into the subconscious mind, and the more likely that they will manifest themselves at the surface. While this is a great aspect of our nature, it can also be a very dangerous mechanism.

The average person spends more time dwelling on the things they fear than on the positive things they want to create in their lives. By focusing on the fear, they create a negative point of attraction that results in negative manifestations. This is how it works: the more thought you put into something (especially if there's a lot of emotion behind it), the more quickly you attract it into your life. The more specific the vision and the greater the emotion, the faster you align to it, going on to discover that it will manifest in your life and/or you'll be attracted to specific circumstances and opportunities to achieve what you desire.

The problem lies in the fact that nothing generates more energy or immediate emotion than fear. Most of our fears live in our heads, and are what we call *linguistic fears*. That means they're nothing more than fears that we think about or imagine, but they generate a tremendous amount of energy based on the emotional charge we put behind them. For example: if you're deathly afraid of losing the one person you love in your life, like your girlfriend or husband, you may notice that you begin to slip into patterns that push them away from you. These patterns may be subtle at first, but they do occur. What begins as loving attention may evolve into smothering, driving someone who was perfectly happy to simply be in your life to the point that they're looking for an exit route. Perhaps instead of smothering, the tactic is to control, which sadly results in creating resentment and anger, all to hold onto a person you cherish.

I'm using relationships as an example because nowhere else is this dynamic easier to spot or does it occur more often. If you can grasp and observe this concept in your relationships, you'll easily see it in other aspects of your life.

This led to a great revelation and turning point in my personal life. In 1959, I was adopted from a Catholic orphanage when I was 16 weeks old. I went home to a wonderful family, including an older brother who had also been adopted from the same orphanage. Everything should have been fine, but throughout my entire childhood I couldn't shake the feeling that I was misplaced, a misfit. In my heart, I always felt I was the oldest child and used to entertain ideas that someone would fetch me out of class one day, tell me that there had been a mistake, and that I was actually the oldest son. I would finally be treated accordingly. This fantasy played on in my head for years, and by the time I was in the third or fourth grade it had expanded into other fantasies of recognition. You see, I truly felt I was misplaced and not properly recognized for who and what I was. I needed attention.

The new fantasies that began to take residence in my mind were fan-

tasies of saving some damsel in distress and being the hero in a potentially dangerous or deadly situation. Looking back, I probably fantasized
about this kind of stuff for hours a day, and why not? My other idea
of being rescued certainly wasn't working. Eventually, the fantasies of
greatness began; I was literally a legend in my own mind.

Forget about Superman and Batman, *I* was the one who would rescue
the cute maiden and get credit. There was a very curious quirk to my rescue attempts, however. In each one, I would either barely escape injury
or would become badly hurt, resulting in the heartfelt sympathy of the
girls. I guess I was having some youthful, preadolescent hero fantasies
of grandiosity and the resulting female attention. Now that I'm grown, I
really think much of this began when my brother and I began to witness
the abuse of my mother and its subsequent impact on our lives.

A curious thing started to happen as I got older. As I began to reach
adolescence, my hero fantasies began to focus more on the aspect of
getting injured and girls giving me lots of attention for it. This particular
phase began after I became a focus of my father's physical abuse. I guess
I figured that if I was going to feel pain, I might as well get something
good out of it (which was the theme of my thoughts, as opposed to the
injuries). In my fantasies, I always recovered quickly, almost miraculously, and oddly enough, this also played out in reality.

By the time I transitioned into a teenager, I started to find myself
having accidents. In very rapid succession, I broke my neck, I broke my
wrist and I damaged a number of other parts of my body. And yes, you
guessed it, I got lots of attention from the girls in my life and would use
it to the fullest extent. Just as in my fantasies, I would heal in miraculous
time. My best friend used to tell everyone that I was the luckiest unlucky
person he knew. Could this have been a coincidence? I never thought
twice about the fantasies I'd been playing out in my head prior to these
events, but they were exactly the same kind of scenarios.

The first set of fantasies didn't have much feeling behind them, apart
from a little sadness. As girls became increasingly important to me, however, I began to have great energy, focus, and emotion channeled toward
these scenarios, and it was only then that they started to occur.

Years passed by before I really made the correlation. In 1982, I was
injured several times in rapid succession. I'm not sure which accident
finally triggered it, but I finally realized that I needed to change my
thinking because it was damaging my body in terrible ways. I started
to think differently, but it didn't keep the bottom from falling out. Yet
another accident struck me, but this time it injured me so substantially

that it affected everything in my life. I was now disabled. I refocused at that point, striving even harder until the accidents stopped. I had finally observed the pattern and recoiled from it.

It was a shame that I didn't figure it out earlier. I was initially unable to stop the thoughts, situations, and circumstances that were deeply embedded and already in motion, but I kept trying. I began to replace and remodel my thoughts, entertaining new, healthier ideas and consciously redefining my beliefs. What's great is that it's such a simple concept, and you can start out small. If you grab a thought and begin to entertain it over a period of time, putting feeling and emotion into it, the subjective mind will start to bring forth the circumstances, conditions, and energy to manifest that thought or scenario and make it possible. You get to decide what you think is possible in your life. You choose how extensively and how significantly you'll allow yourself to change your circumstances by the energy you put into changing your thoughts.

Before you jump to the conclusion that this is "magical thinking" and all you need to do is envision what you want, there is another, crucial side to this concept that we need to address. Not only do we need to change our thoughts, we also need to believe that we're worthy of something better. The greatest desires of our hearts are right in front of us, ready to become part of our lives, but if there's a deep feeling that you don't deserve them, that doubt will effectively hinder your acceptance. You'll subconsciously sabotage the situation because the doubts are lingering signs of the negative inner dialogue you're holding onto. Until you manage to wipe them away, you'll have a barrier up that prevents you from accepting anything positive that contradicts your inner story. It is always easier for us to create the negative because we can relate more to being unworthy.

So how do you tackle this? How do you get out of your own way? Feelings of unworthiness—feeling that you don't deserve something good or better—are agreements and judgments you made with or about yourself, based on the assessments and judgments of others. You created them to define your boundaries in life, essentially defining what you can or cannot have and do. They are limited beliefs that deny the true essence of who and what you really are—an efficient, energetic machine designed to create. They are a lie based on someone else's belief or opinion about you. These assessments did not originate in you—they were handed to you. Have you ever met a toddler that declared they were not good enough to have something they wanted? These are linguistic barriers embedded in you by authority figures through the use of repeated statements or interpretations over time, at an age when you lack the ability to question them.

When I was young, all I wanted to do was play music and sing, but my father didn't believe that was a viable way for someone to make a living. In his mind, you weren't even legitimate unless you had attended special schools and gained an academic education in the field, such as learning how to read music notation. By the time I was 6, my cousin's wife (a music teacher and noted musician) suggested that my parents educate and encourage me in that direction because I had an ear for it. Despite this endorsement, my father didn't agree. Throughout my entire childhood and teenage years, he would tell me that I couldn't amount to anything by playing music because I didn't have the formal musical knowledge.

As I grew up, I learned to play and sing quite well, but noticed that I had a difficult time performing in front of others. I was afraid that I'd be judged and never amount to anything with it. As a result, I continued to sabotage every opportunity that came up, struggling with that inner desperation to realize my dream. I was unable to overcome those linguistic barriers, and one day I simply put down the guitar and stopped working toward my goal. The internal dialogue had beaten me. One year at Christmas, my cousin's wife insisted I bring over my guitar, so I did. I played a number of songs and watched as my father began to cry. The room started to clear, until finally we were the only two remaining. He looked at me, tears streaming down his face, and said, "I didn't know. I had no idea. I am so sorry." Though I'm not certain whether or not he understood the implications, it certainly felt as if he knew that his discouragement had affected me so much that I'd given up on a dream that I'd had a real chance at making a reality.

So, why are you still listening to the stories that hold you back? What's the payoff? That payoff is the real question. It's simple—you get to blame someone else for your lack of success and for your life not working out. You get to remain unaccountable for your life, which makes living with your choices so much easier. If you want to break or eliminate this inner dialogue, you must begin with giving yourself permission to succeed. Even though the dialogue and its linguistic barrier was handed to you, YOU created the agreement to abide by it. Therefore, YOU are the only person with the authority to give yourself permission to go beyond it, and to believe that you deserve what you desire.

Give yourself permission to deserve better. Do this by declaring your value. Observe where you bring value to people, events, conditions

and activities in your life. Recognize, accept and feel these contribu-
tions deeply, and then claim your self-worth. It may cause you to shift
immediately or it might take some practice, but eventually you'll break
through the feelings of unworthiness, neutralizing the negative stories
and their justifications. You will have *permission* to want and obtain the
positive things you desire in your life. You will be allowing yourself
to deserve that which you only dreamt about. This is the **Principle of
Allowance**. Giving yourself permission is to *allow* yourself to receive the
abundant goodness that surrounds you and is waiting for you to claim it.

EXERCISE THOUGHT OBSERVATION

Take out a pencil and paper and set a timer for 10 to 15 minutes so
you don't get carried away. Then, as quick as you can, write down the
different thoughts that come to you in a list. It should be very easy to
fill a page with a list of different thoughts—more than one page is even
better. Now, look at the list and see how many different topics came
streaming through your mind. As you do this, consider how many of
them you actually paused to think about or wanted to think about. Does
it surprise you?

The second part of this exercise is to recall some of the random
thoughts you attach to and entertain in the course of day. List these
on a separate page. Maybe they have to do with grandiosity, success,
unworthiness, fear, disapproval of anything, work, children, discontent,
unhappiness, happiness, gratitude, love, sex, resentment, anger, or any
of a number of possibilities. You don't have to detail the dialogues, just
write down a basic idea of what they are.

Now go back through them and see if you can figure out how many
are based in fear and how many are based in love, acceptance of life, or
other sources. By breaking this down, you can see if you have a generally
positive line of thoughts that you entertain or a negative line. Do you see
yourself as being worthy and having high esteem or as unworthy with
low esteem and poor self-confidence?

Once you've done this, take a look at your life circumstances and see
if your life matches the way you think. Start by trying to link the small
things (negatives are always the easiest to spot). Try to map out the
larger picture and focus on the positive connections. Outlining all of this
in writing is for your own benefit; there is great power in writing things
down, whether you decide to keep it or burn it.

BEING A POSITION

- chapter seven -

What you resist, persists.

"Absolutely not!"

"I will *never* do that!"

Sound familiar? Remember saying anything along these lines, only to find yourself having to eat your words? Or, how about later having to go through with something, regardless of your strong feelings? Maybe there was an outcome you feared, and then ruefully watched it come to pass.

Odd, isn't it? Almost like a self-fulfilling prophecy, or some challenge to the Universe that you lost. Really, what *was* that? How did it happen, or, better yet, *why* did it happen?

So far, we've been looking at the details going on behind the scenes when we create our own realities, and it may seem a bit mystical at first. Truthfully, there's nothing mystical about it—it's all logic.

Let's consider those adamant statements again. They're just a few examples of what I would call an absolute. Absolutes are strong, passionate **positions** we take, whether they're opinions, aversions, fears, wishes, or planned outcomes. Have you ever noticed that when you take an absolute position of resistance against something, it's as if the universe does everything it can to challenge you on it? You could almost say that the very thing you resist finds a way to come into your life and break you. In many cases, maintaining that position results in an outcome that's much worse than choosing to relax and go with the flow.

Another side to this relates to actively working to create or accomplish something. Have you ever set out to achieve a goal of some sort, but no matter how hard you tried, it just wouldn't come together? Perhaps desperation drove you to make the choice to sell out, or maybe you attempted to bargain with God, but ultimately, nothing worked and it was as if everything was against you. What's going on here?

There's a lot about the human experience that we still can't comprehend, but for now, let's focus on what's right in front of us. What we do

know is that the body, mind, and "spirit" are nothing more than an efficient energy center operating in accordance with the mind, coupled with
the five senses. The mind is an incredibly efficient machine that generates
the energy necessary for us to achieve or manifest specific results. While
we can't explain exactly what the mind is, we know it exists because we
all experience it.

When we come into the world, the mind is like an open landscape. In
the beginning, we don't really form attachments to the things we learn,
and they are left to float freely. As we develop and mature, we then
start to identify things as our own and they become personal. We begin
to possess them, we have thoughts about them, and we have thoughts
about our ownership of them. This is heavily supported by the community mindset that surrounds us, which is often related to personal ownership, including the power to control others.

Although the mind is blank at first, it begins to construct a framework
to process the material coming in. One empty area fills with things that
create function in our lives, the other area is dedicated to attachments.
We fill this "attachment" space with possessions—thoughts, objects, relationships, or maybe even incidents in our lives that could be considered
unresolved or incomplete. It's where we file everything we're attached
to—every good or bad relationship, each resentment, and any thought
(good or useless) that we're holding onto. It's incredible how much
clutter we've got in our minds—and I'm just speaking from a linguistic
standpoint.

Now, allow yourself to imagine that each of these thoughts was an
object that occupied a very specific vibration, or portion, of the landscape. We'll call them *fixations*, or **mind objects**. These mind objects
clutter the landscape and may even hold great pain for us, but they're
ours and the ego wants to hold onto them and defend them. Eventually,
it creates a minefield out of this clutter. Some are counter-creative to our
desires, and others we hold onto so tightly that they become our **positions**. These positions eventually become so fixed that we're unable to
create anything in opposition to them. They occupy a space energetically
that we cannot break through until we work them out or let them go.
These objects, like the absolutes, stand in the way of your ability to create
life as you would like it to be.

Imagine that you've purchased a beautiful piece of property on which
to build your dream home, only to be faced with one giant problem. In
the middle of the property stands a large oak tree that prevents you from
doing anything useful with the land. If you really want to build your

dream home there, you'll have to move the tree. Unfortunately, the tree has been growing there for decades and has a deep root system that has networked into a wide area. Even if you cut it down, there's going to be an even greater amount of work needed to excavate the roots before the ground is suitable for building the foundation.

The tree is a *position* that blocks your ability to create or build what you'd like in your life. Though you may be able to move the tree with the help of certain programs that are out there (such as psychology) very few options are available to tackle the excavation necessary to remove and neutralize the roots (the mind objects/fixations.)

The tree analogy illustrates the following: the object (the position) has grown in our minds from a seed—from an event, thought, or con-versation—and will continue to entrench itself the longer it is catered to and allowed to remain. As long as it remains, it is taking up space and requiring care and energy to keep it alive. Doesn't it make more sense to use the space, as well as your time and nurturing, on something you actually want?

A bad relationship might be the event that initiated our position and that now stands in the way of finding new love in our life, but it is the memories (good or bad), the anger, and the personal issues related to the event that are the roots (the mind objects) holding it in place through justifications, rationalization, and living in the past. We often do this by comparing everyone in the present to those associated with the past event. This is where the real damage of being a position occurs, because we're unable to let go.

In cases like relationships, it could go back to the time you were a teenager and your boyfriend or girlfriend cheated on you by making out with someone else. That person may have even been your best friend, tipsy and acting out of weakness one night at a party. Even though it was so long ago, you've had issues maintaining trusting relationships with your friends, especially when they are around your significant other. You also notice that you're attracting people who are cheaters; the reason for this is that the cheating and lack of trust are occupying some very important space regarding relationships.

When you're energetically attracting a partner, you instantly attract someone who is willing to go up against your position, in this case, someone who will probably cheat. You are so focused on what you don't want that you're inadvertently drawing it in. Fortunately, as soon as you come to terms with the position and let go of it completely (including the roots of your rationalizations and justifications why you can't trust your friends around your partner) you begin to attract someone that treats you with respect and dignity, and that you can trust absolutely.

You see, it's a lot like constructing a building. Everything must be cleared from the landscape before anything of real value can be built. I simply can't stress enough the importance of letting go of anything that has caused you to hold onto a position. At one time, I was a position about how many people were tossing their children into institutions because the kids were caught with pot or alcohol or drugs. I was observing a culture of throwaway children. In fact, I was such a position about this that I constantly ran head-to-head with parents, to the extent that my wife and I would end up taking in their teenager.

The teens would do well once they were in my home, but the parents and I always seemed to have issues. The fact was that I was a position about the way they were raising their children, and they were a position about the inappropriate way their children were behaving. In many cases, I learned that they were absent from their own homes as teenagers, and had virtually no idea what being a teenager looked like in a home or family. They were running into their own issues, and as such, ran into their positions and created tremendous impasses with their children. So, they figured that it was easier to put their teens in a controlled environment and let the institutions raise them. I, on the other hand, was being a position about the way they were being raised because I was relating it to my own childhood and the isolation I had felt, including the experience of having been put in an institution for being out of control. As I worked with these teens, I began to work through my own issues and soon had no problem with the parents. I had a pure passion to help the teenagers in a way I wished someone had been there for me when I was young. This led to much of the work I do today, including this book.

In order to really comprehend this, it is important to understand how the creation process works from the very first thought and eventually through the manifestation. It is all about the energy system that we are.

The mind, along with our other senses, is an energy system; each component is a system unto itself, but together they form a refined, efficient super-system of creation and manifestation. Let's think about the mind and how it communicates internally. The first part is the **subconscious**, pertaining to aspects of the mind that control our primary beliefs and functions of the body. Next is the **conscious mind**, which we use to actively process information. That information is communicated using language. The subconscious doesn't need to use language to run the body and its complex functions, but the conscious mind does. In fact, we can even have a dialogue with our conscious mind—the little voice inside of us.

Now that we've established that the energy system we call the *conscious mind* communicates through language, we've also established the **first basis** for creation and manifestation—*thought*. The second is much easier. Once we've thought about something, the **second basis** of communicating is through *visualization*. This is much easier to understand because we all have experience visualizing on a day-to-day basis and the process is very similar to our experience of seeing the world with our eyes. Scientifically, we actually do all "seeing" with our brain; the eyes merely serve to collect data, which is in turn projected onto sort of a screen in the mind.

When we combine visualization with our thought process (which incorporates language) we begin to build energy; we are merging energy systems to create a larger energy base. Whatever the concept that is in the mind, at this point it begins to amass sensory responses such as taste, sound, and feelings. The senses awaken first within the mind and then physically within the body. The more specific we are with the idea, the more awakened the senses will become, and the more senses that can be engaged, the greater is the energy charge for creating our desired outcome.

The more vivid the senses, the more real it becomes, thereby increasing the energy levels. Just like gravity or the pull of a magnet to iron, this energy begins to attract that which is like it. It may be a person, a conversation, information or some other element. If your awareness is such that you realize attraction is taking place and you begin to engage with it, you'll immediately see your idea (which began as a thought) start to manifest.

Basically, the energy that began as a thought elicits an *emotional response*. Emotional responses are charged with their own energy, with a focused intent that affects you and everything and everyone you come in contact with. Have you ever heard of someone radiating with joy or brimming with anger? How do you respond around people like that? Do they draw you in with their excitement or do you go out of your way to avoid them?

Now let's try something. What is the process of building something . . . anything? First, you must have a thought. Once you communicate that thought well enough for others to see it and understand it, they can formulate the drawings to make it happen. Your energy and clarity of vision impact the people and circumstances that will result in this great project or idea. Once the energy has begun to build, funding is found, materials are brought together, and workers begin to construct the idea. This is the same as the internal manifestation process we have been referring to.

As we begin to interact with these elements with focused intent, the thought becomes an object—first existing as an invisible energy, and then as a physical manifestation. It's as if a molecular structure were being drawn into alignment with the idea or thought before we ever took any physical action to create it.

Whether you look at it as an internal process or an external process, all creation begins with a thought, and to have a thought is to engage with language. In the Christian Bible, "In the beginning was the Word . . ." (John 1:1).All things human begin with a linguistic thought or *word*; it is what and who we are. The quicker we realize this, the easier life becomes and we can begin to design our entire life consciously.

In short, when we clear our minds of the positions we no longer want or need, the universe responds by filling the newly open space with what we desire. The only requirement is to get a clear picture of what we want, and then release the outcome to the universe. If we trust it and we are clear about the final result we're looking for, it will materialize for us through attraction.

EXERCISE BEING A POSITION

Write down five things that you've been a position about in your life, and then had to go back on. These are things you might have said you would never do, or someone you swore you'd never talk to or something you said you'd never take part in. Maybe you had to ask for help after declaring you don't need anyone, or go back to a parent for money— basically, anything you took an absolute stand about and later had to retract or submit to.

After you've written these down, take a moment to reflect on what caused you to break your position and how much effort it took. Now ask yourself how you feel about those convictions. Do you still feel the same way or has your position changed? Has your view on things become more open and flexible? That's the real question. What changes have occurred because of the positions you had to give up?

SPACE

- chapter eight -

Space—the final frontier.

Gene Roddenberry likely had no idea how many layers of meaning and possibilities of application could be applied to the statement "Space—the final frontier," when he wrote it. Not only does it have physical implications, it's also critical as an abstract concept. Another phrase you've probably heard is, "You never receive more than you can handle." Guess what? There are spatial reasons behind this truth.

Keep in mind that nothing can be born unless there is first space available to receive it. Basically, no two objects can occupy the exact same space at the same time. (If you're a physicist, just go with that statement for now.)

The same laws apply in the Physics of Communications. You simply *can't* hold two contradicting thoughts at the same time. You may teeter back and forth between them, but you can't possibly have two thoughts at the same exact moment. The mind is so quick that it would seem as if we do hold multiple thoughts in this way . . . but do we really?

The answer is no, at least not consciously. What that means is that before we can create anything in our lives, we must first have space—a blank canvas ready for the masterpiece. It's important to give space to what you're creating so that it has an opportunity to manifest. Many people may want a new car, but it's not until they create space in their lives for one that it actually becomes a reality. I know, having the money for the car is important, not to mention choosing the right vehicle, but basically, if you don't have room in your life for a new car, you will not manifest it. Yes, you can tell me that there are people like Jay Leno who have a collection of cars, but that just means they have space in their life for more cars. Leno has to have room to physically keep them; he actually has a huge building dedicated to his motorized toys. Before that could even come about, however, he would have first needed the mental space to hold such a magnificent vision.

A quick example of this might be if you have ever had an older car that was basically okay, but you just wanted something better. You kept saying, "I'm going to get a better car," or "I want a better car," and then at some point you notice all sorts of things start to happen; you notice the car that you already have begins to run poorly or have difficulties. Up to now, it's always been reliable, so you're not sure what to think. Or, out of nowhere, it stops running or you find yourself, as I did, in an accident. The truth is that the Universe is trying to deliver your request, but mentally and physically, you only have enough space for one vehicle in your life. As a result, the Universe is attempting to clear the space for you by getting rid of the car you have in order to make room for a different one. Remember, you said you wanted a new car, a better car, a different car—not *another* car or to trade up to a better car. Think about the message you sent out. Isn't that exactly what you're getting?

What I'm saying here is that when you want to bring anything into your life you begin by clearing the mind, setting the intent, holding the space open for it to materialize, and only then getting into action. Holding the space open is the trick to creating anything you desire. Holding the space open means that you release all of your beliefs, judgments, and any mental hurdles that are contradictory to what you're attempting to create. If you don't, you'll struggle with it.

Creating space has two basic dimensions. First, you want to clear your mind of negative beliefs and judgments that are contrary to what you're trying to create. Next, you want to forget about it.

I don't mean that you should totally forget about it—I mean let it go and don't focus on what you're attempting to achieve. Just get to work by taking the available actions in front of you and don't entertain any opposing thoughts. If opposing thoughts pop up, just cancel them by realigning your thoughts with your vision. Don't sit there focusing on the object of your desire. Instead, work at being more open-minded and flexible, and release the ideas and beliefs you're dogmatic about. Whatever you do, don't hold a belief or specific scenario in your mind of *how* it should be delivered to you.

The more you practice and learn how to do this, the more effortlessly you'll find the process of creating your life—by choice—the way you truly want it to be. However, you must be specific in your desire and realize that the actions in front of you many times don't have any relationship to what you're trying to create. That's where letting go and trusting comes in.

Let's say you want a new car, but as life would have it, you have no money or job, and the only thing you have planned one day is to help someone move. You work hard to help finish the move quickly and safely, which catches another person's attention. That person figured you did such a fabulous job that they ask for your help with something else, so you agree, because you could use a little money. This ultimately leads to another person who needs help. Turns out, person number three happens to own a car dealership and is able to give you a good deal on a slightly used demo model. When you explain that you don't have the money, he offers you a job and financing off the books, simply because of the quality work you did.

Voila! You've got a new car, even though nothing you did had any direct relationship to the objective. Sounds strange and slightly exaggerated? Well, I've seen things like this happen over and over again. I actually know someone who was given two cars by two separate people—one after the other.

Creating space can benefit us in other ways, as well. If you love someone and show your love appropriately, you give them space and let them choose to come to you; you're creating an environment for a healthy relationship. Everyone likes to know they'll have personal space when they need it. It also provides time for thought and reflection—a chance for the other person to examine how they really feel toward you. If the feelings are mutual, just trust and allow the relationship to take its natural course. If the feelings are not mutual, you should let go because forcing the relationship would only create pain and suffering; you should not attempt to capture them. It's very important to let others into our lives with an open-ended invitation. The only way to do that is by providing space for them.

To reiterate, creating space isn't merely giving them personal, physical space—it is releasing the idea and giving them mental and emotional space in *your* mind, as well. That means you turn it over—clear the mind, set the intent, take appropriate actions that may be in front of you and put it out of your mind (live in the "no-mind" mindset about it). Prayer and meditation can help tremendously with this part of the process.

Space is the very foundation of creation. Take a look at molecular structures—everything around you is made up of atoms. Atoms are composed of electrons, protons, neutrons, and a whole lot of space. The central core of an atom is made up of protons and neutrons, which account for nearly all of its mass. To give you a rough perspective, if you take a 150 lb. person, approximately 149 lbs. and 15.999 oz. would be neutrons and protons (the nucleus) and the remainder would be electrons.

The other primary components of an atom are electrons, which are very interesting indeed. Electrons are essentially packets of energy that "orbit" the nucleus as waves. The distance away from the nucleus depends on the orbiting circumference needed to accommodate the length of one up-and-down cycle of the wave. This orbit is called a shell. Two up-and-down cycles can occur in a shell that is just a bit farther away from the nucleus than the first shell. Electrons completing even more wave cycles will be found in shells for even wider orbits. What happens is that the atom might have a tiny, very dense center, but comparatively big dimensions due to the size of its outermost electron shell. That adds up to a lot of empty space between shells and the nucleus!

For a real-world example, consider this: if you expanded an atom to the size of a football field, the nucleus would be approximately the size of a tomato seed and the electrons would all be the size of a grain of sand.

When you're sitting on the couch, it takes billions upon billions of atoms to create that couch, so you're sitting primarily on space. The idea that it's solid is an illusion. Along those same lines, even though an incandescent light bulb appears to emit a solid light, it's actually blinking at 60 cycles per second. Our eyes do not perceive information fast enough to distinguish the cycles, thereby creating the illusion of constant light. In the same way, a composition of music comprises more than the notes you hear—the pauses between the notes are just as critical. The space creates the platform or stage; it is the structure that supports the vision.

When you begin to understand that the space you clear is the context that defines the content of your creation, you'll have a clearer understanding of why being specific makes such a difference. Creating space is like creating the impression in a mold. Everything works in relation to space, making it a very stable concept concerning the defining principles for life.

To elaborate, context is nothing more than framework. When you construct a building, you first put up the frame as part of the foundation. The design of the frame and the elements within it, like wiring and plumbing, would dictate the mold that the frame becomes. For instance, you shouldn't install a kitchen in the framework for a bedroom because there wouldn't be any plumbing and the electrical wiring won't be appropriate for the equipment. The elements that go into the frame often dictate what content can go in a specific area. You wouldn't frame up a restaurant and instead put in a gym. You get the idea. You must always first set the appropriate context for what you would like to create. The more defined and specific it is, the more quickly life will fill the space with the content you desire.

My ex-wife once bought a $600 queen-sized comforter to go on a bed she envisioned. We couldn't afford that particular bed, much less the comforter, and only had a basic frame with a double bed. When I questioned her sanity, she said she was creating it. She was setting the context of our bedroom and this was her concrete proof of concept and commitment. Every now and then, she would pull this comforter out and look at it to refresh her vision. Then one day, at the right time and place, the money was there and the bed of her dreams showed up on sale in a furniture store, so we bought it. That was more than 20 years ago, and I still have that bed set.

Another good example of this concept is when parents establish the framework for raising their children. They create a context for the child to grow within that is safe and secure. This context is structured or framed by their beliefs, guidelines, and rules, including their observations of other parents they've seen in action. Within this context, the child creates the content as it matures and develops personal desires, experiences, and beliefs. This time, think about your home. If you notice, the furniture and other contents are limited to the context of the environment. If you want to do something other than what the boundaries of the framework allow for, you'll need to reshape the context by modifying (renovating) the framework, much like parents have to do with children as they grow in experience and responsibility.

A number of years ago, my family and I were living in South Louisiana and suddenly found ourselves dealing with a housing situation. Our landlord had passed away, leaving the property to family members who wanted to sell the house we were living in, but there were no rentals in the area and very few houses available for purchase. It hadn't even been six months since Hurricane Andrew had ripped through that part of the state, forcing a large number of people out of homes in the lower-lying areas. We were looking at the prospect of having to go to court to fight for more time or moving from the area completely, which wasn't really an option with my wife's job. While we were out driving one day, my oldest son told us that we didn't need to worry because we were going to find a house that would be perfect. He described the home and the property very vividly. It sounded like a fantasy to us, and we didn't have the heart to tell him that there was nothing on the market, and that we would need a lot more credit and money (that we didn't have) for something matching what he described. After a few days of listening to him tell us about it, we explained the situation to him. I felt horrible about it.

Time was running out, and we had less than a month to find a solution. One evening, the phone rang. A realtor friend of ours called to say she had a house that we should check out after the storms cleared. The skies had been pouring that week, dropping 18 inches in three days, so we figured this was a great opportunity to see if the area flooded, and decided to head over right away. When we got there, we could only see enough to know that it didn't flood, but there was no way we could afford a house that size with three acres of land. Our oldest son was in the back seat and told us this was going to be our new house, the one he saw in his mind.

The next day, we viewed the house in the light. Almost to the letter, it was exactly as our son had described, except that it didn't have a tire swing on a tree, and the siding was yellow instead of blue. Long story short, we got the house. Sometime later, we were doing some renovations and realized that we had unconsciously installed blue siding, and it now looked identical to his description—we had to laugh! Originally, when we broke the news to him that there were no houses available that matched what he described, and that we couldn't afford it even if we found it, he responded not to worry, that he was creating it. I want you to know that he not only created it, but we ended up structuring one of the most creative financing deals I have ever seen, before or since. God is the only one who knows how that house and deal ever went together, but it did, and when it did, this 13-year-old turned to us and said, "I told you." My point here is that a teenager had a greater capacity to create a space for the house of his dreams then we did. Think that's a coincidence?

Four months later and strapped to the plank financially, I listened as my son declared that he was creating that he would get a four-wheeler motorbike for Christmas. He was very specific about the type and model. We explained that the money wasn't there, that we'd spent everything to get the house. However, knowing the power of creation, I decided to put the one he wanted on hold with $50 and see what would happen. Just call it an experiment. Finally, I had to level with him. I told him that I had tried, and even though I put one on hold, I couldn't produce the finances to make it happen. He told me not to worry and that I would be able to get it, but if I couldn't, that was okay, too. He was not attached, and yet he wouldn't accept the idea that it wasn't possible. If I couldn't co-create it with him, he was okay with it. I felt really bad, because the following day it was going to be released from the hold for the next person on the waiting list to get it.

Before leaving to head into town that day, I checked the mail and discovered a distribution from an investment I hadn't heard from in a couple of years. You guessed it—it was enough to get the bike, resulting in a very happy 14-year-old. My family can tell you case after case of incidents like this. If you set the intent, create the space, take the action in front of you and let it go, it's like magic—real magic.

The main point to remember here is that getting out of the way is probably the hardest part of the process. I once heard a story about a man who wanted to have the brakes on his car changed. He found an auto repair shop, walked up to the mechanic and told him exactly what he wanted. After explaining everything in detail, the man asked how much it would cost, and the mechanic answered, "$50 to change the brakes, and $100 if you help." The mechanic knew that there would be more energy expended if the man didn't give him the space needed to do his job properly, so he was willing to charge extra. This also applies to teams. If you don't let your teammates do their job, it creates chaos and performance suffers.

Before we get any further into the chapter, I want to clarify something. I used the term "real magic" earlier, which some of you might take exception to, so I want to explain what I mean. You could say magic is kind of like a miracle—it's getting something hoped for, usually unexpected and illogical under the circumstances, at exactly the moment you need it. It is not David Copperfield making a car disappear and reappear—that's illusion, and there is a difference.

For thousands of years, man has recognized an element to living that's just as real as the mystery of life itself. Everyone has had something inexplicable happen to them, and if the element driving that event could be considered "real" magic, I personally believe it to be the **"magic of believing"**. Cast aside your prejudice and embrace the idea that your life is directly affected by what you believe.

Going back to the topic at hand, you may have heard people talk about the Dynamic Laws of Creation and the book and movie called *The Secret*. Even though it's stirred up a lot of excitement, many fail to understand that before you can actually create what you want and bring it into manifestation, you must clear or create the space for it. This example should illustrate the point very clearly.

One New Year's weekend, I had the idea of doing a little rearranging. I had a friend visiting at the time, and the two of us set about redoing my home office. We rearranged the furniture, and then brought down my son's unused desk from upstairs and positioned it where I thought it should go. I put up a bulletin board and began to stock the desk with office supplies, stepping back periodically to look at it and frame it with my thumbs and fingers like a movie director. Soon, curiosity began to get the better of her and she began to ask questions, trying to figure out what I was doing. I rifled through some files, found the ones I was looking for and then laid them on the desk with everything else. I stepped back again to check it out. Now, she was really curious. Finally, I explained that I was creating the space for my new assistant. I told her that with some of the things going on in my life, I really needed an assistant, and was creating it. She asked about the files and other items I put on the desk, so I explained that the assistant needed work; I was being specific about the tasks I needed her to do. Those particular files contained the things that I didn't have much time to take care of myself and was planning to turn over to this person. My friend was skeptical, and at one point thought I was absolutely nuts.

During the course of the conversation, she bluntly reminded me that I had no money to spend on someone. I politely replied that a particular company I was working with would pay for the assistant because he or she would work for them, not me personally. The tasks I needed the most support on were tasks related to my work for the company, and they would assist me in that respect. She laughed, knowing how that company felt regarding my plans to hire someone on their behalf. Nevertheless, I insisted that it would happen. I stood there and envisioned my new assistant doing the things that needed to be completed.

Two weeks later, I learned that a woman I'd met had been let go from her job. She had good computer skills and was excellent at putting in place complex systems for processing large amounts of information in a very quick, efficient and simple manner. She was perfect for developing the national program we were working on, so I called and invited her to come to work for me and she agreed. I phoned the company, told them about this wonderful individual and a few days later she was assisting me and they were paying for it. My friend was practically speechless after what she had witnessed. This wasn't just a random manifestation, but a deliberate one that began by creating a specific space for the assistant I sought to hire. No matter how many times I witness this at any level, I am always humbly amazed at the power of the dynamic laws of creation and manifestation.

As impressive as it may seem, applying these principles in order to attract the things that you desire in your life doesn't stop there. **Holding space** is one of the most powerful concepts from this book that you can master. Holding space spans far beyond manifesting material objects. It actually ties closely together with the laws of physics, especially in the area of relationships. "For every action, there is an equal and opposite reaction" is nowhere more evident than in the area of communication and relationships. Using the same spatial concepts when you're dealing with others can make all the difference in the world.

Believe it or not, based on this concept, you're responsible for the way others show up in your life. Though most people would rear back and argue with this idea, it is in fact a great truth. The reason most people would argue is because it takes away the "out". That's right, being accountable for the way people show up in your life means you can't blame them if they show up in a way you don't desire. You've set the stage and attracted it. You can't be the victim any longer. I'm not saying you're responsible for others' actions, because you're not, but people that act a certain way will only show up in specific environments, much like a whale may be a mammal but it won't show up on Main Street. It will only show up where there's water. Someone who is rude and obnoxious will not show up in a calm, peaceful, non-reactive environment, because there's nothing to gain from that environment and it has no point of attraction to them.

You have to realize the way that you hold another human being in your mind is crucial to the way they respond and react to you, because it dictates the way you see them. If you hold them in a negative light, you'll only see the negative side of everything they do. If you hold someone as a bitch, then what you'll see is that aspect of that person (though, believe me, we all have it in us). In contrast, someone who holds that same person as an intelligent, warm human being will only see *those* aspects. They aren't blind to the negative characteristics—they just won't have the opportunity to interact with them as much because they aren't "tuned in".

You see, whether we agree with this or not, the truth is that the people we meet or interact with are mirroring some aspect that's in us, and if they're mirroring an aspect that we don't like, it's very pronounced and glaring. It will aggravate and annoy us to no end. The rule here is that we always reflect one of the following: something we are, something we do, something we have considered doing or being, or something we absolutely fear doing or becoming. Unfortunately for many of us, we are surrounded by our reflections. I'll even go as far as to say that we don't notice or give much thought to people who don't reflect parts of us; they're virtually transparent.

While we're here, it warrants me bringing up the idea that we are usually oblivious to our own flaws and behaviors with others. In other words, we may know we have them, but are unaware of the way they manifest. So, when we're projecting our negative feelings and beliefs about ourselves on others, we are refusing to see the wonderful goodness within ourselves. Now, given this as a truth, it stands to reason that when we see and acknowledge the goodness in others, we are seeing and acknowledging the goodness within ourselves even though we may resist that idea at first.

By concentrating on the positive aspects of ourselves, we are acknowledging that we are, do, desire to do or be, or want to become those aspects that we acknowledge. In fact, some level of each positive aspect you see in another absolutely has to be a part of you, or you couldn't see it in them. Given the choice, would you want to see the positive or negative aspects of yourself? An even better question is would you like others to see the positive or negative aspects of you? Why such a silly question? Because when you begin to see the goodness in others and recognize it within yourself in the same way, it brings out more of their goodness when they're around you, and you shine forth with more of your own goodness to others.

One more time, in case I lost you. When you hold a space of goodness for others—focusing on their positive qualities—they become receptive and bring their positive qualities out more and more in your presence. When you acknowledge those qualities in them and they bring forth more of them, they are reflecting the goodness in you. As you interact with them, whether or not you acknowledge it or are aware of it, you begin to see yourself in a light of goodness and you begin to bring out more of your positive qualities with others in general. The innate goodness in you emerges. Their acknowledgement of this through personal interaction brings out even greater levels of goodness in you. Let's illustrate this.

I once had a friend who was an absolutely wonderful human being. Because her family had money, she had been raised to have a certain strong, almost arrogant, way of being that made everyone think she was a real snob. The result was that guys didn't want to date her or get close to her. No one could see the wonderfully sensitive human being behind that impression. While discussing a project over the phone one day, she started to tell me how alone she really felt. She admitted to having a few friends, but that the only guys that would ever approach her were real jerks. I asked her if she wanted me to do a little coaching with her, then made her answer twice, just to make sure she was serious.

I explained how she came across to others and that she denied certain aspects of herself as a result. We discussed the origin of the pattern and her way of being in life. I found her sensitive side and introduced it to her. It was very painful for her to hear everything and to get in touch with that side of herself, but there it was for her to review. I told her to not worry and explained that the perfect guy would be out there. She also had a certain image of what Prince Charming was supposed to look like, and through a process of elimination, I illustrated how she had completely cancelled out 99 percent of all the guys that could ever like her, and that she was unconsciously repelling the rest with her presentation of herself. She had closed off all the space in her life for a real relationship because the guy she imagined would have to fit through a space the size of a Cheerios cereal hole.

Finally, I explained to her that the guy of her dreams probably didn't look anything like she had imagined, and that she was quite possibly passing him every day in the halls at the university we attended or some other place in her life. I explained that she was filling the space she had reserved for "her guy" with that image, and it wouldn't allow room for anything else. I made a few suggestions for things she could do and then we wrapped things up.

Three days later, she called me. She said, "You will never believe what happened!" I quietly smiled inside at her enthusiasm and guessed, "You met someone." Practically jumping out of her skin, she exclaimed that she had.

Before she could say another word, I immediately said, "I bet he didn't look anything like you imagined, and you've been walking past him." She laughed and told me it was true. They both worked in the media center at college, and he had been trying to get her attention for a couple of semesters. Because they had different class schedules, they only passed each other and never worked together. She admitted that she had never even seen him. She was thrilled, and baffled at how it all happened. I explained some of the concepts you've been reading about in this book to her. Last I heard from them, they were moving to Houston together and had great jobs waiting for them.

After so many years of working with people, I see there's no denying that our thoughts are like magnets. We create how people show up in our lives by the way we hold them and the way we hold ourselves, manifesting how people act, react, and respond to us, 100 percent of the time. This spatial concept works perfectly if you can truly shift your thinking to do it. It creates the space for magic to occur. Just remember, the trick is to get your mind to shift to that level of love, neutrality, and peace.

A mentor of mine once got a message that I was having some difficulties. I had come into a little money, and because it was pretty public
in my community, suddenly life changed for me. Everyone seemed to
behave differently and I was falling apart. My friend called to speak with
me and analyzed my daily actions in detail. I couldn't see how I was
doing anything wrong, and he agreed. Then he asked about my conversations with close friends and acquaintances and how I was communicating with them. I replied that I was being very honest about the fact
that I was having some new difficulties. Right away, he knew what the
problem was.

He said I was being too honest with people and letting them in too
far. Actually, I didn't know any other way to be. He explained that I
should be more vague, cordial, and considerate with them, a technique
I was not accustomed to doing. When I balked at the idea, he said, "If
you want to keep getting the same results, keep doing what you're doing. If you want to change the results, change your action." He also explained that despite the fact that I was merely being open, and that my
friends didn't mean any harm, they were unable to keep from wishing
that they had the same or similar problems because it meant having a
little money in your pocket. It was an unconscious thing. It didn't mean
they weren't my friends anymore, it just meant they were human with
natural human tendencies and couldn't separate themselves from their
own desires.

When he explained it that way, I understood and changed my actions.
Amazingly, all the people in my immediate world changed and the
difficulties faded away. Once I understood what the issue was, I was able
to hold these individuals in a different space. By changing the way that
I held them and changing my action, I received an immediate result and
most things went back to normal. This also brings up another interesting
point. Creating the right space (or holding someone in the proper space)
sometimes requires changing your thoughts about them *along with* corresponding actions on your part. The combination of the two instantly
redefines the space, and results become very evident, very rapidly.

Over the years, I've learned that this is one of the greatest truths that
exists. The way that we hold (imagine) people in our minds is exactly
how they show up. Therefore, it's important to always see others with
love. It's equally important to acknowledge and bear witness to only the
good in them and ignore the negative, energetically speaking.

Step away from negative judgments and you'll notice a tremendous difference in the quality of your relationships and the effect that they have on you.

In the beginning, you might notice some differences in behavior that could be negative and cause you to rethink your strategy. Don't waver—this is a natural response from the people close to you. Keep applying this strategy for a short while, and eventually they'll settle in and things will change for the better. It's not easy to change directions when you've been going in a specific direction for a considerable length of time; it takes consciousness. In the meantime, just acknowledge their resistance to change and accept them for it. You're the one changing your perspective, but they'll be experiencing an involuntary change in their reaction and response to you. As we discussed earlier, the ego resists change of any kind that isn't designed to suit its selfish desires.

A woman who came to me for coaching one day turned out to be one of the more dramatic cases I've ever witnessed. She was around 60-65 years of age and was married to a man who had owned a small business for the past 30 years. Technology had changed, and he finally passed the business to one of his sons. Though his son was now the owner, the man would continue to work there every day. It was a very nice, "Cajun family" way of doing things.

During the three decades he ran his business, her husband would come home after work, ask what was for dinner, and then find some reason to start yelling at her. He would argue and scream, and she had hoped this would change after he turned over the business. At first, she rationalized that the pressures from owning a business were causing this tension, which was probably true in the very beginning. After seeing that this behavior had continued, even after handing over the business, she decided she'd had enough and came to see me. I listened to everything intently, and then explained a few of these concepts. I told her that he was getting something out of acting that way, and that somehow her response was feeding him. She exclaimed that she did nothing (which I skeptically believed) but acknowledged my points and concepts. Even though she didn't really understand a lot of it, she told me she just wanted to know how to change it.

I decided to give her a simple task, one of my favorites. Every day that he came home and would try to start something, she should immediately pull out a large pot, fill it with water, put it on the stove and stay there to watch it boil. She asked if she could throw it on him. I laughed and told her no. I reiterated that all I wanted her to do was watch the pot of water come to a boil, and not to leave the pot until he stopped. The idea was to create an open, non-resistant space that would act as a point of self-reflection for him. She thought this was the biggest crock of crap she had ever heard and that there was no way it could possibly work. I told her to give it a shot and watch what happens.

Several weeks later, I got a call from her. She was ecstatic, and couldn't believe what had occurred, especially since she had only tried it to prove to me that it wouldn't work. At first, he would get more aggravated by the fact that she was concentrating on the task. He felt ignored, but she wasn't exactly ignoring him. For a week, this behavior escalated, until he reached a point where he seemed like a lost puppy, not knowing what to do when he came home. For the first time in 30 years, he began to sit down and read his paper until she served dinner. What she recounted bore almost no resemblance to the man she first described. She was so happy, and simply wanted to call and let me know that it worked and to say, "Thank you."

Changing the space in which she held her husband altered her reaction to him, and therefore changed his actions. This process made it hard for him to argue with her because there was zero resistance, and therefore it held no benefit for him. This was an excellent example of the power of spatial concepts in relationships. It is in relationships and in communication that we see some of the largest demonstrations of this principle. It is also a great illustration as to how simply picking up a non-related action and focusing on it can be instrumental in shifting the space.

Finally, I would like to briefly touch on the idea of how we hold ourselves. Oftentimes, we hold ourselves in a certain way in relation to something or someone, and almost every time, we get the results of the space we hold. Of course, the greatest spatial position we can achieve is the space of total detachment or indifference (neutrality) to the results of our endeavors or situation. When we do this, we become transparent, and are not in the way of the highest good coming together for us. It can also be very powerful for us when undesirable things happen in life. I once found myself in a situation where I had to provide protection. It was very dangerous and with a guy who was a known perpetrator. I was simply doing my job and protecting someone.

Even though I had a personal friend there who was very strong and fit, and wanted to jump in, I kept pushing him away. He wanted to protect me because he was acutely aware of the danger, but he detected no fear in me as I stood my ground to protect the person in this situation. Though the perpetrator threatened, made physical approaches at me and explained why I should be afraid of him, I remained completely transparent (an empty space). Finally, the standoff was over and he walked away.

My friend first asked me if I was nuts, and then quickly asked why the man didn't assault me. He wanted to know how I could simply "be there," seemingly without any fear. I told him I wasn't a space to be hit. I further explained that I had no fear because I knew I wasn't attached to any specific result other than to protect the situation by not moving. Therefore, there was no fear at all and I wasn't a space for the bully to hit. Each time he started to hit me, my lack of fear and resistance stole away the results (fear) he was looking for, and therefore he could not hit me. The absence of fear left me very peaceful inside, despite his threats to move against me. I have done this sort of thing many times in my life in different kinds of situations. I recommend understanding it well before taking it to this level, but it does in fact work. We've all witnessed people who can show up to an out-of-control situation, and their presence just seems to calm everyone down. It's the same thing.

It is a known fact that the people most likely to get mugged put out specific body language that gives the muggers the idea they can get away with it. Someone who has taken courses in self-defense (changing the way they hold themselves) is seldom mugged. It is all about the way you hold yourself in your mind first and body second. If fear is present all around you, you'll attract reinforcement for those fears. You will validate them.

Space is an incredible concept that few of us recognize we have the ability to influence, and yet it can be such a powerful tool. From the very beginning, the way we hold ourselves dictates the situations and conditions we attract. From that point, the space in which we hold others will determine how they show up in our lives and finally, holding the right space will always determine what we attract in our physical life.

Space truly is the final frontier of human development. When we actually learn to master this concept, we'll be able to do nearly anything—from creating the life we desire to creating world peace. Whether navigating relationships or working to manifest the objects of our desire, creating space is one of the most powerful concepts we can apply in our lives. In fact, it is essential to mastering the Art of Flow. Always remember that everything began as simple energy being introduced into space.

EXERCISE CREATING SPACE

Want to really put this theory to the test and prove it in your life? Take something that matters to you that you own, but don't need, and give it to someone who needs it more than you do. Very keenly observe for a while and you will notice that the energy of the gift comes right back to you and fills that space. You might give away a coat or a pantry-full of food you never use. You might not see it come back in the same form, but if you are keen and observe closely, you will see that it has been replaced. You will notice some things that simply just show up in your life, like money or something else that you desired. In fact, it may be something that you couldn't get before and couldn't figure out why. Suddenly, it's right in front of you and it's yours.

On the other hand, you can simply clear space in the garage if you want another car or clean out your closet if you want new clothes, and then do what is in front of you and watch how the opportunities lead you to what you desire. No, it probably won't magically appear, but you will be led by following the actions in front of you to what you desire.

It is a good idea in this second scenario if you write down exactly what you are clearing space for and then put it out of your mind.

Caution: I absolutely do not encourage you to give away something you can't do without (like your car) on your first time doing this. To receive the return quickly takes practice and trust, and that takes time to develop. For now, just simply do things that are small or manageable — things you can observe easily. The idea is to create space and watch as the universe fills it.

SHOWING UP

- chapter nine -

On the road of life, there are passengers and there are drivers.

You may recognize that slogan from Volkswagen ads, but part of what makes it so effective is that it registers on such a deep level about life in general. There's nothing like the exhilaration of getting into an amazing machine and taking charge of the road, and life is the same way. It is imperative that we are conscious in our lives. If we don't see this, we're cutting ourselves short.

What happens all too often is that we tend to only pay attention to the bare minimum needed in order to get by. We become minimally present—you could even say that we "check out" until something wakes us. There's an ebb and flow to each day—routines and conversations we've been through a hundred times, interspersed with occasional situations that require a little more focus. We become complacent, living our lives in a waking sleep. We spend more time in our heads with fantasies, daydreams, making plans, and reflecting on the past than we do fully aware of the life we're actually living here and now. It doesn't have to be like that.

Showing up is simply being **present**. To be present, you must be conscious, open-minded, and ready to be of service. You voluntarily become an active participant in your own life through choice and accountability, and carry that outward to the community. When you show up for the things that are important to you, great things can happen.

Showing up is something that others expect of us, and by doing so, you'll grow in a forward direction and win the respect of those around you. If you avoid it, you'll be **diminished** (by both yourself and others) and find that those very people may not support you when you're in need.

Many people show up in some areas of their life, but are completely absent in other **domains**. I've always shown up ready and willing to coach people, but couldn't show up to write, even though people had been asking me to do so for years. I absolutely trusted that insights would come through me while coaching—that I had a gift for verbalizing things—but I didn't trust that I could transfer that into writing. I didn't want to be judged for my writing and was allowing my insecurities to hold me back. It wasn't until I bought a magazine franchise and needed to write a publisher's letter every month that I had to confront what was happening. That's when I realized my writing could have just as powerful of an effect on people as individual coaching. Ultimately, the thing that usually keeps us from showing up is fear—fear of the unknown, fear of being judged, fear of not being good enough, or fear of failure—and I was no different.

Showing up breaks down into two categories: First, you have to show up for yourself and second, you must learn to show up for others. Although slightly paradoxical, showing up for others, no matter how you do it, is one of the first steps in showing up for yourself. While it's important to realize the effect your presence has on those around you, it's even more important to get out of self by learning to move your own ego out of the way and trust your inner guidance. In other words, being more concerned for others' well-being or something higher than your own little mechanisms and ego-based desires is of tremendous value from a personal standpoint. It's an easy principle to apply when you figure out just how important showing up is in every aspect of life. How you show up determines the life you live because it reflects the level and direction of your commitment. The results you get in life will be proportionate to the commitment you bring forth to live it.

Commitment to something is important and very powerful. You are showing up when you've learned to honor your commitments with integrity. Does it matter what you show up for? Not really. Anything that you're willing to stand up for and care about is good enough. In a piece called *The Master Game*, by Robert De Ropp, the author speaks about engagement. He goes on to say, "Seek, above all, for a game worth playing," and "If life doesn't offer you a game worth playing, then invent one—surely, any game is better than no game at all." To me, he's talking about showing up in life and finding something that matters to you. Find a game, create a game, but make sure you show up and play. This is what's important.

I've never forgotten the way one of my mentors illustrated the idea of showing up. For years, I'd been suffering from the disabling injury I mentioned in an earlier chapter. I would lie around every day and sleep till noon, and then stay up and watch TV late into the night. I didn't do much of anything. Over breakfast in Nashville one morning, he asked me if I had enrolled in college yet, and what I had planned now that the litigation was finalized. I told him that I had kind of sort of made a decision to go to college. I'll never forget the next few minutes. He immediately put me in my place and explained that no one can "kind of sort of" do anything. He told me to go home and sleep all day, like I'd been doing, and call him in six months to let him know how far that had gotten me. I got pretty humbled in that moment. I told him I would sign up at the local university as soon as I got back. The analogy that he gave me next changed my life. He said life was like a ball game. There are people who are on the field playing, there are people who are on the sidelines trying to get into the game, and then there are spectators in the stands, just watching. He made it very clear that I was trying to be one of the spectators viewing the game safely from the stands.

He pointed out that the problem I was running into, and would continue to run into, is that life is not a spectator sport. He drove this home. Either you're in the game, playing your heart out and enjoying the results of your actions, or you're on the sidelines, dealing with the consequences of your non-actions. No matter which one I chose, the game was going to keep running. I had to decide if I was going to jump in the game (go to college) or let life pass me by (view the game from the stands). That morning, he got me to realize that it was fear keeping me in the stands, because I was afraid of losing and being judged. Being on the sidelines *guaranteed* I would lose. If I jumped in and played, I would at least have a chance to be a winner.

A semester later, I humbly informed him that I'd made the Dean's List. He responded by telling me that was pretty good for someone who was afraid to show up, suit up, and get in the game. Since then, I've never forgotten how crucial it is to show up.

I may not feel like participating sometimes, but it's the only way to play. In fact, when I confront most of the things I fear and don't want to show up for, those are inevitably the situations that rarely go as I envision, yet bring me some of the most beneficial experiences in life. I'm positive that you can relate, if you really think about it. The things we fear and resist the most often bring us the greatest lessons and rewards.

EXERCISE SHOWING UP

Find someone who really needs something. It could be a group or someone you know, or better yet, a stranger or group you're not familiar with. Maybe what's needed is help, maybe it's money, or maybe it is just a friendly ear to listen for a while. Without any concern for yourself, put aside any limitations you have or anything you've got going on and simply be of service to that individual or group.

Sure, if they need money you could help them by donating, but that doesn't really count. What you need to do is go out and help them raise money or show up to help them in a way that will bring value to their efforts. For many Americans, giving money is one way to absolve ourselves of guilt for not showing up. We simply throw money at a problem, but that only does so much. There are specific times when it is better to get engaged with other people. Go help feed the homeless at a local mission and you will quickly see my point. Next time you buy all the fixings for a big dinner, make a choice to have someone help you find a family that has nothing and give it to them while you go do something different. It just might be the best day of your life.

You show up for yourself when you show up for others, so do something that matters. Do something tangible on a personal level and you'll know that you've made a difference.

PRINCIPLES OF FLOW

- chapter ten -

The idea behind the Art of Flow presented itself while I was completely focused on developing a new workshop. At the time, I had just finished the Alan Cohen Mastery Training and a 40-day water and green tea fast, and was working on my personal energy in the realm of dating—Law of Attraction kind of stuff. I had a lot of information to process from these experiences and wanted to put together a workshop that embraced the concepts of my coaching technique. That's when the initial concept of *flow* came to me.

The idea isn't complicated. It's like placing yourself in a stream and allowing the current to lift and carry you exactly where you need to be in life, and trusting that every single experience is perfect in every way. This is the hard part, but it's absolutely worth it. Essentially, you are emptying yourself of attachments from both the past and present in order to create space for new, more powerful demonstrations of things that you desire. Despite its simplicity, it's not easy. It means to live a life based on non-resistance and maintain a state of no-mind. For most of us in the Western world, this goes completely against what we were taught growing up; it is an exercise in allowing and trusting the process of life, without resistance or attachment.

When I began to review how "flow" fit in with my experiences coaching others, I was awestruck at how it made perfect sense. I suddenly had a deeper, more elemental understanding of what I'd been doing for years with clients. You could even say it was an elegant solution.

The first thing I did was review the themes that invariably come up when I'm coaching: love/relationships, sex/sexual aspect of self, and religion/spiritual dimension of life. As these three areas came into focus, I studied how I coached each one. I knew there were patterns, but this time I was attempting to deconstruct them to their basic elements. With each theme, I noticed that the primary tactic was to break down the barrier or point at which the person had hang-ups in order to create a breakthrough for them. It didn't matter which one they struggled with—the process was always the same. Once we discovered the issue, my primary job was to guide them in a way that allowed them to take what was now a blank canvas (created by removing the issues) and replace it with a mindset that was more conducive to ongoing change and growth.

No matter what the issues, how we arrived at them, or how traumatic the experiences that surrounded them, the process was almost predictable. In fact, it was so similar that I was baffled—especially once I realized how little I really did. It dawned on me that I was only the facilitator and that everything else happened during that person's interaction with their internal self. I was primarily there as a supportive party, neutral observer, and a guide to new possibilities. I was the articulate one, available to help with the communication process needed to make these things happen.

There was also a pattern to overcoming issues that would come up *after* the breakthrough and a way to empower people to move on in a more fluid manner. It was the idea of being fluid that caught my attention; I was teaching people to flow in life, rather than resist it.

After decades of my own experiences battling against life, I finally learned to stop fighting. I observed that life has a certain rhythm and flow to it, and that despite my best efforts to force things, life would always work out better if I simply did my part and *stayed the hell out the way*. My mother had been right when she said that I was my worst problem and worst enemy. It was the constant struggle against life that brought me so much grief and pain. I wanted control; I wanted life to favor me, give benefits to me, and give me an advantage everywhere I went. I believed in limited supply, which meant I wouldn't get mine if someone else got theirs. Your winning took something away from me.

There was so much there. At first, I resisted the idea that I'd been wrong about so many things in my life, but then I loosened my grip and let go. I realized it was okay to be wrong, because it gave me power and the freedom to release all the ideas about myself and about life that I held onto so tightly—the very things that imprisoned me. Admitting this gave me a sense of open-mindedness that I can only relate to as being completely *fluid*.

During a conversation we were having, a friend of mine said he realized he needed to be flexible to be successful at life. He brought up flexibility several times, like it was his new buzzword. Finally, I broke it to him—flexibility implies bending, and bending creates tension. Anything with enough tension in it will eventually snap or wear out. I asked if this was the effect he was looking for, and he promptly replied no. I explained that he could learn to be fluid and flow with life, rather than bending and resisting it at some deeper level. It was an eye-opener for him. I went on, saying that if you observe anything in nature that is truly adaptable, ever-changing and all-embracing, it would have to be in a state of fluidity.

Liquid does not resist anything natural—it merely goes around it, over it and in some cases, through it over time. It is not upset or stressed at being stopped or dammed up for later use; it sits patiently and adapts to its environment. It holds no tension, even though it can be put under pressure. He was just astonished, but immediately started making his own identifications regarding the concept. The next day, we spoke and he told me he'd already been telling other people about it.

This may not seem like much at first, but being specific about the way we hold things and the terms we use to describe them is very important and can assist with the flow of life. I've also learned that if I make my declarations, sit back, and do whatever action is in front of me, life will bring everything it has to offer right to me, as if it were on a river. I don't need to go upstream, chasing what I want; I need to be patient and let it come to me.

Personally, I've noticed that the only time I actively pursue what I desire is when I want things my way or am unwilling to wait. That's an attempt to rush the process, trying to force life to hurry things along by fighting against the current and swimming upstream. Conversely, I chase after things downstream when I'm living in the past and want to recapture something that's already drifted by. In this case, I'm usually in fear that I've missed out on something, that I let it pass out of reach, or that I didn't get everything I could have gotten. I'm just not willing to let go—similar to when someone you know dies at an early age.

You see, I've learned that this flowing river moves people and things in and out of my life at a perfect pace. My job is to utilize the experience of them to the fullest while they're present and then let go as they pass. I don't need to fight or force, and I don't need to hold onto anything or anyone. If it's meant to be back in my life, then it will return at the right time. Perhaps you've noticed this with a relationship you thought was over, then suddenly you find it right in front of you again, somewhere farther down the road and probably better. The funny thing is that life is like a stream flowing towards us, while at the same time we are also one with the stream. Another way to put it is, *"We are the observer, the participant, and the stream itself."*

This profound concept explains so much for me. As a spiritual being having a human experience, I am the observer and participant. No one else has the power to take action in my life and utilize the gifts that the stream delivers to me. It is my responsibility and choice whether or not to gather joy, wonder, love, harmony, and balance as they drift my way. If I choose to battle the current, it will mentally, physically, and emotionally wear on me. If I cling to the edges, afraid of flowing with the stream, I begin to die a slow death because clinging is not living, and attempting to live in avoidance of fear is absence of life and love. Unfortunately, the latter two concepts are what most of us choose to do. We resist life and hang back at the edges, instead of embracing it and learning to flow with it.

The stream is what you could call your mind, conscious, subconscious, and God consciousness. It's the way I interact with my mind that determines what I create in my life and how I create it. In other words, I create or call forth what the stream provides or delivers to me by the way I think and interact with my thought process.

If I interact with thoughts of negative beliefs, my focus is on the negative, and I'm setting myself up for negative experiences or opportunities for negative experiences. It's what I'm tuned into and geared up to tackle, so that's what I immediately latch onto in nearly every situation in my life. I see the glass as half-empty and have an attitude of being a victim, so my interpretation of things will be skewed towards the bad, even when there's no real justification for it. You've probably met a few people who somehow see the worst in even the most wonderful situations. In contrast, if I think positively, cleanly. and without mental clutter, I'm setting myself up for opportunities to have positive experiences.

We've all seen the people around us who seem to do no wrong, as well as people who seem to do nothing right. You know who they are. Stop for a minute right now and recall how each one tends to speak. I am willing to bet that one stays in a positive vein of thought and the other tends to speak negatively. Realize that the difference doesn't lie in the words they say out loud so much as the thoughts behind those words.

You may be thinking about someone you know, a wonderful person who does all the right things, such as go to church, volunteer, or be a great friend, but always has problems and major obstacles in her life. On the other hand, maybe you're thinking about this really snooty witch down the street who doesn't do anything for anyone but seems to get all the spoils. Right, I know this seems like a great injustice to you, but in actuality, if you listen to both of them very closely, you'll notice a tremendous difference in the way they think, especially how they think of themselves and how they hold life.

"Sally-do-good" may think that (according to her religious views) God is testing her with difficulties. This is her belief. Have you ever noticed that people who believe in a testing God are always being tested in some way? Just as we've illustrated, you manifest what you believe in order to validate your belief system and yourself. On the other hand, maybe Sally simply doesn't think she deserves a better life, or that to live a good life you have to struggle. Details aside, I assure you that by listening carefully, you'll discover a dialogue in Sally that will absolutely coincide with her life experience as it stands.

But what about the woman down the street? She is brusque, dominant, seems cold and closed off, and is not involved in the community at all. If she didn't have children, no one around the neighborhood would even know she was there. So why does she get everything she wants, but Sally doesn't? Once again, you have to look at the dialogue within the individual. Maybe she believes she's worthy of making great achievements, having a wonderful, prosperous job, and receiving everything great and beautiful that life has to offer her. In this case, that's exactly what would happen. Her success is based on how she thinks and the dialogues in her head. The singer Jewel has a song lyric with the line, "To be forgiven, you must first believe in sin." This woman has no contrary beliefs, and therefore materializes things in her life very easily. She doesn't believe that you have to be this great community volunteer, religious patron, or giver of self to earn your way to prosperity and abundance. If she did, her visible experience would be substantially different.

None of this may seem right from where you're sitting, but it *is* complete and perfect justice; each woman is determining the framework of the life she wants, according to what she's thinking. Invariably, you're likely to be more adept at navigating those paths you've been mentally training yourself to handle and are prepared to deal with when the time comes. Would you choose to enter a marathon if you hadn't been training for it, or would you decide that viewing the race from the sidelines was good enough? Would you have invested the time and energy in training if you didn't believe that you had it in you? If you don't believe you're good enough, more than likely you won't stick with the program to achieve the result, no matter how much you entertain yourself with ideas of athleticism or the satisfaction of achievement. You have a belief that is determining your path.

If you want to know how someone thinks and what their primary dialogues are, pay close attention to the patterns in their life. You can even do this with yourself after you become good at it. Any recurring pattern speaks to a given mindset; someone who has problems finding love is more likely to have a mindset that they're not worthy enough for a deserving relationship. You might deduce that there are self-esteem problems related to feeling a lack of worthiness. Or, perhaps they see themselves as better than everyone else and subsequently, no one is good enough.

Once you see the patterns and know the personality, you can then map them to your own experiences, using your emotions. At this point, you can pretty much hear the dialogue in their mind. The concept of mapping it to your personal experiences using your own emotions and/ or thoughts is very effective once you realize you wouldn't be able to see their issues and problems if you didn't have something in yourself that could identify with them. Using this process can always give you a fairly accurate idea of someone's mindset, as well as your own, because you can only recognize those things for which you've already made distinctions, and anything beyond that is transparent to you.

As you begin to develop a flow mindset and wrap your head around the idea of being fluid, you'll begin to call things into your life with increasing speed. The more you practice and trust the process, the more rapidly things flow to you. The more you let go and allow life to easily move things into and out of your path, the more natural the idea of fluidity will become; you find that you're no longer resisting, either consciously or unconsciously. This can take some time, but it's well worth it. Allowing life to develop around you is what it's all about, though it takes great trust in the process for it to become second nature.

Though my own life has been quite an experience and could certainly testify to the development and efficacy of these principles, I realized that this concept was so huge that I needed a broad canvas to illustrate it, something that would be easy for people to accept, understand, and trust. I knew that I needed to have an example that would be very accessible, and found myself studying the life of Jesus—not what he taught, so much as how he lived. I discovered that if there were ever a person who embraced being fluid and was the master of flow, it was him.

After two years of research, I arrived at a simple outline of how he lived, centered on eight principles that he seemed to predominantly live by. I compared them to the six key points that I'd already arrived at from the flow concept and found what I was looking for—overlapping principles that work and guide us to a joyously fluid experience in life. It would seem that the six principles of flow were nothing more than a condensed version of his eight. I also realized that these same principles are common to many philosophies, religious groups, and programs, but are simply covered in different ways. I've come to the conclusion that there is no new material—just new ways of presenting it.

The principles that I identified are Love, Forgiveness, Acceptance, Gratitude, and Open-mindedness, applied through a sixth principle, Truth. In other words, there are universal truths (just as there are laws in physics) and there are personal truths (which unfold when we apply specific principles). The result is that we begin to see our purpose in life unfold and realize how events, conditions, and circumstances fit together for our higher good. Once this happens, we become fluid and trust the process, so life begins to flow naturally. It isn't long before we see the results of this way of life.

We start to detach from fixed objects and concepts and move freely in a new rhythm. Life begins to serve and support us in a wonderful way— peace and harmony becomes ours. We begin to see the bigger picture in life and align to a personal groove in a way that is uniquely ours. We become the individualized expression we are meant to be within the greater experience of existence.

Below is a list of the two distinct sets of principles. The first is the set of principles Jesus lived by and the other is the set of principles I teach in the Art of Flow.

JESUS' WAY / THE WAY / THE TAO

Without Resistance / No Mind / Detached

Trust

Forgiveness

Love

Gratitude

Acceptance

Humility

Truth

THE SIX ESSENTIAL POINTS OF FLOW

Love *(Unconditional Care for Others)*

Forgiveness *(Honesty & Accountability)*

Acceptance *(Non-resistance, Trusting & Without Judgment)*

Gratitude *(Humility & Affirmation)*

Open-Minded *(Space & Detachment)*

Truth *(Accountability, Humility & Acceptance)*

If you look beside each of the Six Essential Points of Flow, you'll notice that I've placed in parentheses the actual principles by which Jesus lived. Though some of the flow principles may be a combination of some of his, the underlying concepts are the same. Times may change, but the actual "rules" to a happy, healthy life are non-negotiable. Love, acceptance, and forgiveness are the key catalysts in a successful life. These three work together, hand-in-hand, to create a space for open-mindedness, truth, and gratitude.

LOVE

- chapter eleven -

One element—through the act of giving—grows ever more abundant,
and that is LOVE

No subject in the history of mankind has so captivated us, command-
ed so much attention, or inspired so many pieces of artistic expression as
love. It's elusive—constantly drawing us to pursue it and align with it. It
lingers in our dreams. It beckons like a drug. For some of us, it *is* a drug.
We may seek its illusive effect, only to become addicted and forced to
search for replacements when the initial high wears off.

Think about the intense emotions that often characterize the beginning of many relationships, consuming to the point that people can
barely think of anything else. Storybook images come rushing forward,
driven by entrenched hopes, dreams, and years of programming. We
enter a microcosm of feelings and one-sided perceptions. The world is
bliss, the stars shine brighter, and all of life is perfect and in divine order.
It is undiluted, captivating, and all-consuming.

Passionately entwined in emotions, a couple may spend weeks,
months, or even years in this condition, but eventually they will reawak-
en to reality and the business of everyday life. Maybe what they felt was
an awakened state (though limited in perspective), but the time will
come when they go back to "sleep" and look toward outer things to sus-
tain that feel-good experience, even though it may entail stepping away
from the relationship. The drive to maintain the emotional highs of love,
happiness, and joy are indicative of an addiction to the brain's drug-
like hormonal euphoria that is associated with falling in love. When the
euphoria stage settles down, many assume that they've fallen out of love
and feel they're now trapped, with no way to receive their fix. They may
get a divorce, break up or seek another person in an effort to reacquire
those feelings, oblivious of the natural stages of healthy relationships.
They aren't seeking true happiness and love; they are pursuing illusions
and extreme emotions—a heightened sense of what they call reality.

If those highs aren't love, then what is? Honestly, that discussion's been going on for centuries and analyzed by more knowledgeable and enlightened people than me, so I'm going to leave it alone. What I am going to do is present a few different ideas that you can ponder for yourself.

Some consider love to be an emotion, one that presents us with certain feelings that we react to. Love makes us feel good, at least in our minds—therefore we *are* good. There are also those who categorize love as an action. Essentially, if someone treats you in a loving way and you're compelled to reciprocate, then you're experiencing love. A number of years ago, I was hosting a group coaching session and one of the guest presenters brought that up; I almost fell out of my chair. Up to that point, I didn't give a lot of consideration to the idea that not everyone experiences the world through their emotions the way that I do. It brought me to an awareness that we define our world and things like love based on our dominant senses. I noticed in my friend's presentation that everything had a very visual and action-oriented approach to it. In other words, he had to see visual evidence of everything in his world to truly grasp it.

You've probably heard people say that they're auditory, visual, or kinesthetic learners. If you ask a person who is primarily auditory to visualize something during meditation or a hypnosis session, they may not be able to acquire a trance-like state. This is because they can't connect or relate through that visual sense. Their method of observing and interpreting the world is different, and so their ability to visualize without aids may be much weaker, preventing them from being able to "see" a particular item or scenario in their minds. In the field of hypnosis, hypnotists read scripts during a session that are written specifically for different issues and treatments. When writing a hypnosis script for a given treatment or prescription, it's necessary to capture all three aspects—auditory, visual and kinesthetic. Similarly, it's perfectly logical that not all people experience love through the same primary sense or define it in the same way.

After hearing my friend speak, I realized that I tuned in to love from an auditory and emotional perspective, but wasn't big on the visual aspect. In other words, if you told me that you loved me and then gave me affection, it would stir my emotions and you'd have me. Guess how well that worked for me—it didn't. That's the reason I was attracting women in my life who were insecure, great at affection, freely and frequently spoke the words, "I love you," but then treated me very poorly. They were just responding to the space that I provided for them. That's how I perceived and received love, so naturally that's who showed up to fulfill that need in me. My idea and space for the type of woman I desired was very off because it was based on those magical feelings most of us assume to be love when we develop a new relationship. It was more of a high that I was receiving from personal validation.

When a woman found me acceptable, it validated my ability to be loved and give love. I was 10 feet tall, bulletproof, and all was well with the world. I mentioned attracting insecure women; when a woman had certain insecurities, I would feel strong, acceptable, and play the imaginary role of the protector in my mind. In this way, I would get the same feelings associated with being validated, because it made me feel like a real man. Once again, this all came from an internal sensation or emotion without any real action or physical evidence other than the fact that they were with me. However, people are often where they are because they are paralyzed with fear for one reason or another and not because it is truly where they want to be. This is one of the things that lend great credibility to the action concept.

Armed with the knowledge that I lacked an action-oriented perspective, I began to consciously show love through actions, while voicing it less. The difference was staggering. I began to attract completely different women. I also noticed that if I treated myself in the same way, it made a huge difference in how I felt about myself, as well as the people that came into my life. It was a way of filtering out all of the individuals who did not resonate with that way of being. Suddenly, people who were more balanced and selflessly cared for themselves began showing up.

So, how do you experience and process love in your life? Do you do what I did or do you have some other combination of elements that you use? Don't limit yourself to what I've described here—your personal experience of love is uniquely yours and no one else's. The power lies in knowing how you interpret your reality of love, which can only come from living in the question of how you process your world. Then, you'll be able to easily embrace new ways to bring forth love in your life. The broader our ideas and methods for interfacing with love, the greater the level of love we seem to be capable of comprehending. The way you believe it to be is the way it will show up for you. Subjective mind makes that guarantee.

Now that we have the romantic kind of love out of the way, we're able to focus more on pure, undefined love. Undefined, meaning you sense it, feel it, speak it, act it, and embrace it because it "just is." It is a way of being. It's the part us that is completely unexplainable, yet infinitely wonderful. It's not the love that sonnets are usually written about or what you might hear on mainstream radio. It is the love that we experience deep inside ourselves, and often relates to something greater, like God or Spirit. If someone is in a healthy relationship, this is the kind of love that will show up with time and a receptive partner if we're not lulled into blindness by the ego through routines or by complacency.

To put such an enigmatic, unexplainable concept into words is very difficult. Love is. It really needs no explanation, but for the purpose of our discussion, we'll define love as *unconditional caring for others*. There are two problems with this definition to keep in mind: 1) it leaves no real space for the idea of self-love and 2) most of us are incapable of experiencing love at this level with any consistency. It means a total absence of self and putting other people's needs above your own. It drives home the idea of complete trust in something greater than ourselves: God, Spirit, Destiny, or a Divine plan. This definition leaves no room for compromise. You're either unconditional or you're not, and unconditional means complete abandonment to the idea of caring for another, no matter who they are, what they've done, or what they do. When Jesus died on the cross, he didn't say, "God, condemn these sinners!" No, he said, "God, forgive them." He accepted them without reservation. That's my understanding of what true love is—complete acceptance of others without condition or judgment. This is what makes forgiveness so key to a successful life filled with love.

Outside of childhood, most people have never truly experienced love. This is simply because they're incapable of totally abandoning themselves to it. As they grow up, it becomes conditional—*I love you as long as you do such and such*, or whatever condition might exist. On the flip side of things, a lot of people can't experience love because they have no basis for distinguishing true love—they don't really love themselves first. That is a strong assertion, but nevertheless very true in some of the coaching I've done. They're equating love to the euphoria I spoke about earlier, or worse yet, to acceptance from others. That becomes an issue because it means seeking approval by proving ourselves worthy of their love in some way that is probably not who we are as part of our core being. We begin to compromise, hiding our true self in order to receive their approval and acceptance. In return, they express love to us, so we continue the pattern of losing ourselves in the process and wind up developing a poor skill set for love and relationships.

This would mean that everyone I claim to love in my life (to the point I became conscious or awakened) was based on some set of influences or interpretations that developed into a belief system at what was probably a young age. These systems then built judgments to wall off the outside and protect my belief. If you followed all of that, then you realize that for anyone to reach a true level of pure love with you (short of your children) is extremely difficult. Our belief systems and barrier of judgments make it difficult for anyone to get past all of our insecurities to truly develop an unconditional love with us. Love doesn't know judgment and condemnation—love *is*.

If you can't get past judgments about yourself in order to first fall in love with *you*, how can you get past them to love someone else? Even more, how can anyone else get past them? Whenever someone looks at you with love, if all you can see is the version of them that was filtered through your beliefs and judgments, how can love at a core level really exist between the two of you? When they tell you how wonderful you are and how much they love you, do you bring up judgments about yourself and about them regarding what's being said? Be honest. Not many people that I've ever met can see the wonder and beauty that their lover sees in them, at least not from an authentic perspective without the ego.

Ego is not love. In this case, it's merely an inflated opinion of ourselves that helps us feel better about who we are inside. The truth is that we're not bad and we don't need ego to conceal the "bad" for us. That's only a belief. The idea here is to see yourself in the eyes of God or Good or Love. When you can do that, you may see who you truly are, not some childhood image of the bad or imperfect person you believe yourself to be. You are perfect. You are the perfect expression of yourself, the perfect expression of God as yourself. When you begin to see this, you'll start to accept everything about you, and love will follow. When I coach individuals or do workshops and witness the moment this "clicks" for people, a spark ignites in their eyes. They'll tell me later how they never really knew what love was or hadn't ever experienced true love since they were small children. You are perfect, whole, and complete.

Let's get back to the explanation of why most people haven't experienced true love since childhood. Because we've established that judgments and belief systems keep us from connecting at a deep level with others and that we're all one, it stands to reason that any opinion, judgment or condemnation that we have towards another is a reflection of ourselves. In fact, it's usually something that we are, that we're afraid of becoming, or that we've been. If we cast judgments upon others, we're casting judgments upon ourselves—individually and as a unified body. If we're judging ourselves harshly, we cannot love ourselves, and therefore can't experience true love. If we're judging others harshly, we cannot experience love with them. It works in both directions.

Finally, because of our interconnectivity, we cannot judge ourselves without judging others and we cannot judge others without judging ourselves the same way. This comes under the cycle of karma. What we put out to another we must get back, because we attract what we think and speak. That being the case, how can we really experience true love if we aren't first living in a mindset of love and forgiveness? This means we must love and accept ourselves completely before we're capable of loving others.

In the Lord's Prayer, Jesus illustrated that he was aware of that truth by putting in what some refer to as the "spiritual trap". It states, "Forgive us our trespasses as we forgive those who trespass against us." He knew beyond a shadow of a doubt that to be forgiven, we must first forgive, because if we can't forgive others, how can we possibly forgive ourselves? This is crucial to reach a state of pure love. If we can't love and accept ourselves unconditionally without judgment or condemnation, how can we possibly love others unconditionally, and vice-versa?

Throughout this chapter, you may have noticed that I didn't measure love by degree or address the different forms, such as being in love, love for a child, or love for a spouse, mother, friend, or church parishioner. Love knows no degrees; it is simply love. It's only the coupling of distinctions that make it different. For instance, *being in love* is more like infatuation coupled with love. That's not a bad thing—it's just a clarification. To a parent, love has no boundaries for their children, and vice-versa. Regardless of their actions, loving or otherwise, instinct mandates that we love our children. We may not be proud of them in certain situations and they may upset us, but nevertheless, the love deep within us can't be eliminated, because the fundamental truth of love for them lives within us, as does the love for a parent. It exists, regardless of circumstance.

When I was in my mid-20s, I truly believed I hated my father. I tolerated him because for some reason, he was the one person from whom I needed to receive approval for my life. I needed that acknowledgment to feel love from him. One day, I was notified that he had cancer. I didn't get to clean things up with him before he died. I was a little rattled and felt very set up by a stepmother who put all the expenses and funeral arrangements onto me. Fortunately, my uncles were present to guide me.

After it was all over, my mentor and I were playing golf one day and I was expressing some resentment and anger at the situation. He explained that one day I would see that it was the greatest honor I could ever have to bury my father with dignity and honor his life in death. It was something I took to heart, although I just couldn't see it at that time. Later that year, I began to forgive my father after attending a workshop and suddenly, love came flooding in, like it had been there the entire time, waiting to be released. Once this tremendous flood of love came through me, I experienced exactly what my friend had said. I now knew it to be the greatest honor in my life to grant him that final dignity. All of the other things no longer mattered. I can say I forgave him and mean it. I experienced a real freedom from the resentment and anger I had held onto for so long.

What I learned through that experience is that once love is established, especially between a parent and child, it is a bond that is forever present. We may stuff it down with hate, resentment, and anger, but it does not die. It merely waits for us to be awakened and let it come forth. No matter what the condition, circumstances, or situation and no matter how we describe it in degrees and levels, the one consistent factor is unconditional caring for another. The terms we use to describe love and heartfelt feelings are merely distinctions to define conditions surrounding that love we feel.

Jesus was one of the greatest men to walk the face of this Earth because he mastered the concept of love and forgiveness and the way they work together. He understood that there cannot be and is no separation amongst mankind. Each one of us is a part of the other. We're like a massive organism, entwined together and completely interdependent. To deny this fact of life is to break flow and struggle against the current. Some people may seem to make that work for them in business and in their lives, but it's what you don't see that really matters. In most of those cases, you don't actually want to look behind the curtain. Without truly knowing or understanding why, we're designed to work as one. We operate best as a single body and are able to create and accomplish things very easily when we're unified. Have you noticed how many movies show someone beating the odds by embracing community and receiving support? As varied as lives may appear from person to person, on a fundamental level they are considerably similar. After two decades of coaching, I can tell you that there simply isn't much that makes one person mentally and emotionally different from another at a core, instinctual depth.

Think of the ocean and all of the creatures and organisms that inhabit it. It amounts to a vast array of species, but they're still part of one living entity known as the sea. If that precarious balance becomes disrupted, the devastation would quickly spread to every level. We're connected in a similar manner, but on a more subtle, virtually undetectable plane. We are interconnected and interdependent, strung together in networks. Whatever way you look at it, make sure you grasp this concept and how it affects living and interacting with others.

EXERCISE LOVE

Sit in a quiet space and write down in one column those that you love and have felt love for in the past. Please be generous and truthful in your listings. In a separate column, write down the qualities that made you feel such great depths of love for them. This would be the part of this person that you viewed as being special and good. In yet another column, make a list of all the good points within yourself that you love.

Once you've done this, compare the list of good qualities you loved in others with the good qualities you love about yourself. You may notice, if you really look hard, that many are the very same qualities. However, for many of you this will not be true. It won't be true because you've trained yourself not to look at your good qualities because you don't believe them. If you don't believe them, then how can you say you love yourself?

Now, go back to the column of good things you loved about the other people and read through them, but before you do, write the words "I AM" in front of each one. This is correct. Everything good you see in others *must* live within you at some level, because if it didn't, you *could not* make that distinction. If you love someone for that quality, then you must possess it yourself, or you would not and could not love them for it.

Now that was the easy part. Part two is a little more difficult. Go into the world before you read the next chapter and begin observing people in stores, in cars, in malls, at work, or wherever, and make a choice to only see the good in them. Focus only on the good in each person. This can be quite difficult if you're not used to it, so it might take some practice. As you observe those qualities, quickly express gratitude and thanks for having that quality within you. In doing this every day for a short time, you'll notice it becomes automatic and you will quickly notice yourself giving thanks for who you are, forgiving your shortcomings, and simply falling in love with the wonderful, perfect being that the Universe has created you to be.

FORGIVENESS

- chapter twelve -

To err is human, to forgive divine.

Forgiveness is a decision—a resolution—that happens within us. It often requires forgiving ourselves before we can forgive others, and it enables us to release the bonds that have chained us to a person, event, circumstance, or situation. In fact, you could say that forgiveness and freedom are synonymous.

To help grasp this concept, think about the paradox that when you accept something you wish to be free of, you're finally able to release it (surrender facilitates winning), or that the more love you give, the more love you have to share.

Many people believe that forgiveness is something you do for others—granting them a pardon for their actions and behaviors. They truly believe that it means giving your blessing and permission to the offending party or event. Actually, if I'm honest with myself and think back on almost any event, I invariably find that I've done something, said something, or put myself in a place for that event to have occurred. One of the examples that spring to mind is when I wrecked my car on the Interstate. It wasn't anyone's fault and no one else was involved, but I was driving and decided to be where I was in that moment. The weather facilitated the accident, but I was the one responsible for the choices that led to placing myself in that position at that exact moment. I was out in poor weather, driving a car with tires that were a bit worn, and for some reason I changed my mind when I was about to turn off, resulting in losing control of the vehicle. Immediately after it happened, I was there in my car starting to get angry, but caught myself, accepted responsibility for my actions and went through a forgiveness exercise so that I could release it right away. Soon, I felt better and was able to move on before the police arrived. I could simply embrace the event with gratitude that no one got hurt and I was safe.

The reason forgiveness is so hard for many of us is because it requires tremendous honesty and accountability. We live in a world that teaches us to cast blame and that being wrong is a bad thing. This sets us up for all sorts of discourses (including avoidance of accountability), so it's no wonder people have problems with forgiveness—accountability is a critical component of it! Until we can begin to see things honestly and take responsibility for our own lives, we can hardly achieve forgiveness. We must be capable of objectively assessing our own condition, actions, and situation. In addition, we also become answerable for the way we perceive and interpret others' actions.

We have to see our role in events, including the influences that cause us to look at things the way that we do. Many of the incidents that people need to be forgiven for are not caused intentionally, so I know that the problem is often primarily due to my own interpretation of what happened. Perhaps their words or actions triggered my insecurities, making it seem threatening to me in some way and all too easy to interpret as intentional attacks. In reality, I need to forgive myself, first and foremost, before going on to forgive them. If I forgive myself first, I notice that I'm much more receptive to forgiving the other party. It's a method of self-accountability. We simply forgive ourselves for our part and then everyone is clear and clean.

As Jesus so clearly pointed out in the way he lived, no matter what they did to him, he remained free inside—in his heart, where it counted. In this way he was untouchable, and demonstrated it by forgiving those around him and praying that those who wronged him be forgiven. He knew this highest of spiritual concepts—that one must forgive others openly and freely to be free and discover the heaven he spoke of on Earth.

So, how do you get started? First off, it's important to identify your role and your feelings about placing yourself in the path of the event. I know this doesn't fit every situation, but it does fit a fair share of the messes in most of our lives. For those things that we clearly didn't have anything to do with, we need to find a different level of forgiveness; praying for the willingness to release them is very helpful. However, and I want to be very clear about this; if you find yourself in one of those completely random events in which you have truly been a victim, you'll probably notice that you're most likely blaming yourself at some level for the event. Forgive yourself for condemning yourself, even if all you can manage for now is to forgive your reaction to the event, condition, or circumstance. Next, find a method of matching your process of life with the other party's process of life, so that you can put yourself in their shoes and possibly understand why whatever it is may have happened. This is simply trying to understand or find a connecting point as to why they might be the way they are and act the way they act, as well as why they do the things they do. If you can relate your life to theirs, it will be easier to forgive them.

Many times we don't want to release the other party because it means we'll have to release ourselves. There seems to be something internal that insists we rake ourselves over the coals for things that are merely random, just as a child might feel that they are to blame for their parents' divorce or financial troubles. It is so simple, and yet so difficult! Many of us want to dwell on our pain until it becomes so devastating that it chokes us and steals the very air we need to breathe. To forgive would mean to release these issues. Let me clarify.

A parent that loses a child to a drunk driver would ultimately be devastated, and rightly so. Like a virus, anger and resentment can quickly become all-consuming, and it doesn't take long before their destruction focuses internally. While at first the anger may be directed at the drunken party, it wouldn't take long before it turns inward. The parent may be blaming themselves or beating themselves up, thinking that if only they had done something differently, the event might never have happened. It is human nature to turn the blame inward and make ourselves "pay." This is a perfect example of a time when forgiving ourselves first would be crucial. By forgiving ourselves and finding the love and self-consideration in this situation, we would be lubricating the wheels of forgiveness of the other party. The prayer states, "Forgive us our trespasses as we forgive those who trespass against us."

This one little phrase holds so much meaning! Of course we would forgive ourselves as we forgive those who trespass against us, because we're using the same mind to forgive both ourselves and the offending party. What you may call God or the Universal Creator is something that is infused within each of us, as well as within us collectively. If this is true, and we are asking for forgiveness, then this force can only provide forgiveness to us to the extent that we can open ourselves up to forgiveness. For example, if we ranked forgiveness on a scale of one to 10 and we only opened up enough of ourselves to forgive at a four, then our ability to receive forgiveness, whether from ourselves or another, would only be at a four. That's because we're receiving forgiveness from the Universe or the God Mind through a mindset of a four. You cannot contain a gallon of water in a quart jar. Do you get the picture? Forgiving ourselves completely opens us up to a greater degree so that we can forgive others more completely, which ultimately releases us at a deeper level. We are creating a larger space for it, thereby opening ourselves to experience a greater demonstration of forgiveness.

These are key elements to bear in mind. We are, in fact, one Universal Mind. We are the expression and existence in the physical realm of a Creative Energy, or however you choose to label it. When you act out upon another, you are acting out against yourself. It's counterproductive because the same divine energy in them is in you, so it's safe to say we are one.

When we act out against another, we are acting out against ourselves and the whole of humanity. In other words, to not forgive another is to not forgive ourselves—both parts of ourselves—personally and collectively. When we forgive ourselves, we're not only forgiving our own person, but are also forgiving the collective, thus clearing the path to forgive the other.

To practice self-forgiveness, we have to be completely honest and stop perpetuating the ego-driven belief that we are the other person's victim. When we hold them as the perpetrator, we are playing the victim and no release can be found. Victimhood is weakness; accountability and ownership is power. Would you rather stand in weakness or in your personal power—the power of choice? When you hold yourself as the victim, you're stating that the other person has stripped away your power of choice and now controls you. If you don't believe me, try mentally stopping the anger. If you're honest, you probably can't, because they own you.

By holding yourself in the position of power through the act of accountability (known as forgiveness), you set yourself free. You take ownership for your experience, even if it's just the experience of what you feel about the person, situation, condition or event. Either way, it's still you standing in your power. It is the beginning of freedom. Anger, resentment, and hatred are so consuming that they will take up as much of your energy as possible if you let them. They'll also prevent the flow of life from running smoothly and create chains of events and circumstances that you don't want in your life. When you forgive, you open space for life to flow. This is the most important principle in this text—creating a space for our lives to effortlessly manifest what we desire.

If you don't forgive completely, you begin to close off parts of yourself and create repeating patterns. Whenever we deny things like forgiveness, we're inadvertently setting up opportunities that force us to see it. Life will create situation after situation to teach us how to forgive until we finally get it. This is the real horror of holding a grudge. Years down the road, we look back and think, "Why have all these negative things been happening to me?"—only to see them completely stop once we've learned the lesson or process, which in this case would be forgiveness. To reiterate, if you have someone you are not willing to forgive for whatever reason, then very quickly you begin to block off a part of the collective self. This requires energy and takes up space for the personal self; it becomes fixed, like the furniture in a room. At times you may even move it around, but you'll notice it's still right there. These are the things you don't want to release. They require so much energy and space within you that they impede the act of creative manifestation in your life. You can intend and desire and allow all you want, but the Laws of Attraction will only bring you a version of what you want that matches the space you have created to receive it. It is that simple. The space and the energy wrapping that space will completely dictate the experience of what is manifested in your life. It is similar to the karmic principle, "You reap what you sow."

Have you ever noticed that construction crews take weeks to replace a bad section of road? They rip out the old material and spend a tremendous amount of time fixing the substructure and preparing the ground until it is a perfect foundation for the new road. If all they did was cover up the old road with a new layer of asphalt, any cracks or inadequacies in the original road would eventually undermine the structural integrity of the new road. The old cracks would work their way into the new layer and you'd be back at square one. You also wouldn't try to build a skyscraper on a lot that's only big enough for a convenience store. The area of the base wouldn't be large enough to provide a safe foundation to support something that big. It is important to ensure that the foundation of your design in life is solid and spatially adequate for what you intend.

Forcing something to manifest in a space that isn't large enough or ready to support it simply doesn't work. You have to deal with what was there in the first place before something new can stick. You have to deal with the baggage. When my ex and her husband came to live here after Hurricane Katrina, it was open-mindedness that opened the door, but it was forgiveness that cleared the space for redefining our way of being and interacting. It required an initial willingness to forgive them, and then a willingness to forgive myself for my participation in the way things were. Finally, I had to forgive myself for the mindset I had towards them. Forgiveness was the only means to successfully clear away the wreckage of the past I was holding onto and the only way to expand the space for manifesting a greater future.

It is all about energy. If all things are made up of energy and we are a dynamic expression of energy, then it stands to reason that our thoughts are charged with energy in a way that affects how we create our lives. When I used to think that forgiveness was for the other person, not for myself, I didn't like the idea that it was endorsing their behavior in some way or that I was agreeing to take the loss. Eventually, I realized that forgiveness was for me, and that each time I forgave someone, it created tremendous change within myself. I began to think more clearly, act with greater decisiveness and have more mental and physical energy. I discovered that forgiveness shifted me to a more positive mindset, releasing me energetically.

I once had a girl I lived with for a while in my late teens. She was the Cinderella story in my life. After meeting her in passing one day, something just clicked and I knew that I loved her. I found out her name and where she was from and told a friend that I would drive to her town to find her. He laughed at me and said, "No way." Running all over the countryside and with nearly 100 miles behind me of trying to gather information and track her down, I found myself knocking on a door. Much to my surprise, she was the one who answered. We were inseparable for the next three years.

We were young, but we were very much in love and fit well together, at least for a while. When it ended, I felt horrible for the way I acted with her and for things I had said and done. I didn't know any other way to be; I had a very poor background when it came to interpersonal relationships, and had been on the receiving end of a lot of abuse by that age. I brought my lack of interpersonal skills into our relationship and destroyed everything that we had together. She was the primary victim of my abusive nature, along with the drinking and drugging of my youth.

For years afterward, I desperately wanted to make amends to her, but felt that it would do more harm than good to show up in her life. I knew that the fear it would incite in her wouldn't be offset by my humble attempts to make up for what happened. I felt horrible and needed some resolution. I prayed intensely about the situation and to finally be able to let her go; I was now married, but still so in love with her. I began to have dreams in which the two of us would have a conversation, but would wake up before I could make amends. After a year or two of these dreams, one night I finally stayed asleep through the dream. I made complete amends to her, followed by a heartwarming conversation and parting with a loving hug. I woke up instantly. Things were different.

I spent the next few weeks in a blissful state of relief, knowing that it was all right and I had achieved resolution. I had somehow said everything I needed to say to her and got the full benefit in my waking state, as if it had happened in person. Although I still loved her deeply, I had lost that infatuated, "in love" feeling. I had released her. Dreams have always been a very powerful tool for me, but this was unimaginable.

She had not gotten any benefit from my dream that I know of, but my apology and our mutual forgiveness of each other within the dream freed the bindings that held me to her for so long. Although I was married, I had not been able to give my wife 100 percent, because my heart wasn't completely free to do so. After that experience, I had freed up the space to really fall in love with my wife.

Forgiveness allows us to find inner resolution so that we're able to move on; it addresses and resolves the baggage left inside of us from various experiences. Jesus was the great purveyor of this message. He knew the truth. He was aware that staying in a constant state of resolution allowed us to be detached and free, inside and out. It empowers us energetically, enabling us to continually create our lives in an ever-expanding way—mentally, physically, and spiritually/emotionally.

Forgiveness is the true path to love and personal freedom that gives us a way out of our negative past experiences. It allows us to free up much-needed space to create new and wonderful things in our lives. Clearing away the wreckage, forgiveness gives us the capability to experience greater depths of love and accountability, a key to expanding our consciousness. It is that increased consciousness that allows us to enjoy greater experiences in life. Forgiveness is the key to a life filled with joy and wonder.

EXERCISE FORGIVENESS

Many years ago, a very special woman, nicknamed "B," taught me a forgiveness exercise that I would like to share with you. This is the exercise I use to this day. It is made up of a three-stage process and requires the repeated use of each step (especially in the beginning), but works incredibly well.

I forgive _____ for _____ as I know _____ forgives me. I now release them and let them and this event go with love and light.

I now forgive *myself* as I know my Creator (God, Spirit, the Universe, etc.) forgives me. I now release me and let "me" go with love and light.

I forgive God (My Creator, Spirit, the Universe, etc.) as I know that God (My Creator, Spirit, the Universe, etc.) forgives me. I now release and let go of this person and/or event.

I've made my own modifications to this process over the years. Each time I say it, which is nearly every day (*if we're honest, there is almost always something or someone to forgive*), I simply imagine white light wrapped around the person or visualize balloons carrying the person and/or issue into the sky until I can no longer see it. When I am finished with everyone and everything for that day, I simply repeat, "It is done."

This is one of my favorite processes and it works really well. I invite you to begin using it. If you are doing it regularly, you'll notice that you wake up one day and as you search for something in your mind to forgive, there is nothing, and the noise in your head is quiet. It is a wonderful feeling.

ACCEPTANCE

- chapter thirteen -

Acceptance is the key to the elimination of all pain and unrest.

In the beginning, we have no comprehension or understanding of resistance. Life is a vast experience, to be observed, absorbed, and accepted without condition or reservation. As infants, we discern little more than the difference between comfort and discomfort—our reactions dictated by instinct and the drive for food, rest, security, warmth, digestion, and elimination. We are soaking up input while creating our framework for life. We accept and do not judge.

Our framework for filtering the world—the "rules" we've observed and strung together—slowly begins to evolve into beliefs. We transition from simply discerning our comfort level to associating words (linguistics) with our preferences. With each new experience comes a new distinction, followed by a new belief, and with each new belief, a new preference/judgment. We begin to determine judgments from a standpoint of the ego, rather than instinct, indicating that we are constructing the substructure of our personality—the *self*.

We use our preferences to determine what is or isn't acceptable according to our personal standards, morals, and beliefs. But are they really our personal standards? Many of the things we hold as ours actually came from our parents, various authority figures, and the community around us. When we're very young, we need help filtering and interpreting the experiences we encounter, and their "help" winds up influencing the foundations we develop our lives upon.

Our ego becomes ever more developed with each new set of beliefs and subsequent judgments, and we determine what is acceptable and not acceptable based on its insecurities and fears. As time goes by, our critical faculty becomes increasingly rigid and we develop a natural acceptance and/or resistance to what is and a strong desire for things in life to go our way, according to our beliefs. We begin to buy into the illusion of separation and knowledge—the "I know" mindset.

Quite simply, the "I know" mindset is in effect when we start believing we have the answers to everything around us, despite the fact that all we actually know are perceptions, based on our judgments and beliefs. We are no longer an observer of the experience of life. Once we believe we know, then there is little to no room for learning. In fact, this way of being is supported by parents and the community around us, especially the educational community, which *expects* us to know.

For many, this powerful illusion puts us at the center of our own universe and eventually, in collision with the world surrounding us. We live in the answer rather than the question, and may develop a certain "I know" attitude. Living according to this ideal, our desire is to be in the right (based on our programming) and we'll often go to nearly any length to uphold it. Maybe we're seeking to control our environment, maybe we desire feelings of security, or maybe we just think that we're supposed to know all the answers, so we pretend to know them. On the other hand, maybe we've been convinced that we had to be right because something was wrong with us if we weren't. In any case, we find it difficult to accept things that don't correlate with what we want or the way we see them. We spend an enormous amount of energy "being right" and positioning ourselves not to be wrong. There is a difference. For whatever reasons, with this behavior we are usually avoiding being accountable.

In some cases, we are right by the standards of the community. Community standards are ideals that we, as a unified social body, agree are for the good of everyone from a social perspective. For instance, murder is wrong, robbery is wrong and driving while intoxicated is wrong. These are things that have been categorized as harmful to the greater good and are considered unacceptable. We might also find ourselves in a personal situation that's unacceptable, but that allows us to believe we are right and happy. But do we really get to be happy because we're right? Probably not. Even though we may very well be right, we're still resisting what *actually is* by not accepting life the way it is, and wind up creating more problems for ourselves.

Here's an example. A young boy was killed by a drunk driver. By any interpretation of our community or personal standards, this is wrong, and there can be no justification for it. I won't deny this to be true, but rather than take a position about it, I freely accept it, knowing there's a greater good involved. In this case, the mother of the child decided to take action, and as a result of her child's death created an organization called MADD (Mother's Against Drunk Drivers.) She changed the legislation regarding drinking and driving. Her loss was great—no one can dispute that—but her effect on the nation as a result of the death of her son was nothing less than remarkable. The accomplishment doesn't take anything away from her loss, but it does illustrate a greater good at work.

My point is that I could spend all my time stuck in being a position about people who drink and drive. I could be angry, self-righteous, and belligerent about this condition, or I can accept it and free up my energy by not resisting what is. To do this, it's necessary to have a certain amount of trust and faith in a greater good, although at times we can't see it for a while. Please don't misunderstand me. If I see someone wanting to drive after they have had too much to drink, I am responsible to take action and stop it, if possible. I'm not endorsing it, just accepting the condition that already exists.

I was out driving once (and being very conscientious, because it had just rained) when I suddenly felt the back end of my car dancing around. I felt the traction going, and a moment later I was in a spin. The car spun around in the road and hit the center wall on the Interstate, coming to rest on the median. Fortunately, I wasn't hurt and had miraculously avoided three lanes of traffic. Everything got handled and I was soon picked up and driven home.

Several days later, I learned that my car was totaled, and the amount of the compensation for the loss of the car being given to me was almost equal to what was still owed on the car. I was upset at first, but then I accepted that this was simply the way it was, and getting upset wouldn't help. I had no credit, no cash in the bank, and not much income, yet was only mildly bummed out. I knew in my heart that there was a bigger picture that I was unable to see in that moment. Being aware that I was immersed in the situation and that everything looks very different when it's all happening to you empowered me to let go of the realization that for the first time in 33 years of driving, I was without a car. I knew this could adversely affect my personal life as a single father with an active teenager, as well as my business. Even though the situation looked rough, I held strong to my faith.

Soon, I got a call from my oldest son and he told me that I could use his SUV until we were able to work something out. Someone else offered to keep their new car at my house in case I needed it. You see, the answer was very simple, and only my resistance to accepting this situation could keep me in pain, because everything that I needed was provided by the people around me. The only requirement was for me to show a little humility and accept their generous offers.

The more we hold on to things, as opposed to accepting them, the more emotional pain we create for ourselves and in some cases, the people around us. Our pain is in exact proportion to our resistance to change. Change requires acceptance. We must release the things in the past and make room and space for the new. Acceptance is the key to happiness. When we don't accept what is, we are in a constant state of fight, depleting our energy and the resources needed to live with health and happiness. When we refuse to acknowledge that everything is perfect and exactly as it should be, we become stressed and vulnerable to illness. In some cases, we become alienated from those we love. We become cold and unaffected, and lose the sensitivity that keeps us authentic and connected with those around us. We lose our capacity for intimacy and love becomes a distant concept that we believe is great for some, but doesn't work for us. We attract people who are obstinate and self-righteous, or people that we can control because they don't have a backbone in order to stand up against our obstinate and self-righteous behavior. To our detriment, we surround ourselves with support and validation for our rigid beliefs. We develop an entire support system for remaining unaccountable and living a life of resistance.

I once coached a fifth grade teacher who was an absolutely fabulous woman. Even though she had been at her job for 15 or 20 years, she hadn't lost that compassion, understanding, and desire to make a difference with kids that so many of our teachers lose along the way. She'd been married for about 20 years at the time and her husband had a debilitating disease that was progressing very slowly and caused him a great deal of pain. They knew it would one day take away his ability to work and be financially productive, and every day she dealt with his pain and bitterness due to his unfortunate lot in life. He withdrew emotionally, stopped touching her and talking to her and showed almost no affection, leaving her without any sense of connection for many years. She loved him very much and wanted so badly for him to wake up and just be grateful for the life they did have, instead of focusing on the pains of the disease and what it would eventually do to him.

I worked with her for several months and during this time, an opportunity to be intimate with a man she used to like in school presented itself. She was flattered by his approach and spoke to me again and again about how she felt and what to do about her dilemma. On several occasions she asked my opinion, and I encouraged her to do what was in her heart. I assured her that everything would work out the way it was supposed to if she just followed her heart, but that I couldn't (and wouldn't) give her the endorsement that she wanted so badly. I did, however, give her a very realistic outside perspective of her situation and explained to her that she would not be a good or bad person either way. I reassured her that if she needed support in either direction (regardless of her decision), prior to or following an upcoming high school reunion they would both be attending, I would be there for her. Finally, she made a decision and went through with it.

We spoke about the event several times, and while she felt very good about her decision, she wanted to share it with her husband. I reminded her of what I had told her beforehand, that if she did this, she would probably be looking to free her conscience at her husband's expense at some point. Nevertheless, she still wanted to do it. So, I told her about a program and asked her to attend it for a weekend first. I explained that I thought he would go if she did, and then they could have that conversation and it would reduce the chance of him being hurt by her experience. She agreed to do it.

Several weeks later, she went through the program and as expected, he followed. I ran into them at a program function quite a while later and she introduced me to her husband. Much to my surprise, he grabbed me and hugged me and thanked me for everything. He said that she had explained everything and he was so grateful to me for being supportive of her in her endeavor. He further went on to say that because she did what she did and followed it by going to the program, that he felt alive again and that they had their life back as a couple. I heard how they now had an intimate life and how she would never have had the courage without the support behind her. The two of them were on fire and they looked amazing. He was alive and seizing every moment he had with her and with himself. He had given up his resistance to the cards life had dealt him and chose to embrace life instead. The results were fabulous. I would not recommend or endorse someone doing this, but it certainly worked in their case and had a tremendous positive effect on both of them.

If we become willing to accept accountability for the things in our life and give up on resistance, whether it's a position that we're stubborn about or the self-righteousness of our belief system, life will begin to serve us and we can live with vitality, joy and love. In the Art of Flow, we give up our positions and righteousness; we give up our fights in life and we become fluid—acceptance, allowance, and receptivity become our anthem. We live with purpose and ease, detached and knowing that all is well and as it should be in the Universe at any given moment. This is the key to freedom.

We can do only one of three things in any given moment:

Accept what is (*embrace it*)

Resist what is (*fight it*)

Allow what is (*surrender to it and be without resistance*)

In these states, we can be clear and take effective actions that can make a difference. We can see who we are as well as our current situation, and we can assess things from a point of neutrality. We can take action without attachment and have clear choice.

EXERCISE ACCEPTANCE

Reflect back on things that may have mattered once upon a time and that somehow resolved themselves. Write them down and see if you can point to the exact moment everything seemed to work out. See if you can pinpoint when the acceptance came to you. If you're honest with yourself, you may find that things didn't clear up until you finally let go and accepted the condition you were resisting.

This is often very easy to observe when there is something that we really want. You want it very badly and you just can't seem to live without it. One day, you finally resign yourself to the idea that you may never get it. You accept your life without it, and then suddenly, it is right there in front of you for the taking. It was the acceptance that cleared the path for it to show up in your life.

See if you can list actual accounts where you observed this happening in your life. In fact, think of something you have been wanting for a while. Forgive yourself for not having it and then release it. See if the opportunity to have it shows up shortly after you release it.

GRATITUDE

- chapter fourteen -

"Any day you make a list of 50 things that you are grateful for is a day you will not be depressed or sad" — Bert D.

In the concept of flow, if **open-mindedness** is the river bed and **acceptance** is the fluid nature of the river, then surely **love** is the mass, **forgiveness** is the rate at which it flows, **truth** the direction and **gratitude** the increasing momentum over distance (Momentum = M × S × D). Gratitude is the only true discipline that can be practiced in the Art of Flow. All of the other elements require additional factors to be a part of their application. You can go through the motions to forgive, but it's not until forgiveness reaches a deep level of acceptance that it takes effect. Truth can be practiced, but as stated before, it is only capable of showing up for you in proportion to the vessel prepared to receive it. Each of the elements in the Art of Flow requires some form of inner acceptance before they become realized in you. Gratitude, on the other hand, is like prayer—you don't necessarily have to believe it for it to be effective. Just go through with the action; the results always follow.

In coaching, one of the most effective tools I use with clients (especially ones having trouble making a breakthrough or with issues they're afraid to face) is to make a list every morning of things they're grateful for, without becoming mechanical and duplicating it every day. Start with things that you can feel or see (that are close to you and are the most tangible), and then work your way outward to broader things. As taught by Abraham-Hicks, I believe the process needs to start before your feet hit the floor—not always an easy thing to accomplish. This assignment has great power in it because it begins your morning on a positive note that sets the tone for the rest of the day, similar to the way a musician might use a pitch pipe to tune up before a concert. It's a highly effective method that works with great results.

Once I explain this to clients, I instruct them to buy a notebook or journal and write a letter of gratitude at the end of each day; hopefully, as the last thing they do before going to sleep. They can write the letter giving thanks to Spirit, to God, or to themselves—it doesn't really matter. They are to give thanks for their day while expressing their gratitude for *everything* that happened. Most are quite amenable to this process from the start. However, when I tell them that they are to especially give thanks for the negative or bad things that happened to them, they usually freak out and begin to debate me. The real purpose of this exercise is that we should be grateful for *everything* in our lives, because we don't understand how each one affects us. Giving thanks for the good things lubricates the mind to give thanks for the things we perceive as negative.

Let's say you're a business owner and you lose your business and home as a result of some unexpected event, like the people affected by the 9/11 disaster in New York. You might think that surely that's the worst thing that could possibly happen to you. Six months later, you find yourself living in a new city in a new state, opening a new business with no money. Life is tough. You break up with a woman you love and respect dearly. You struggle for a while, but then start to get on your feet again. One day, while helping another person through a difficult time, that individual encourages you to write a book that can potentially affect hundreds, if not thousands, of people in a positive way. You've heard that before, but for some reason it's different this time. So you write it and set up workshops to teach the material. Looking back, was losing your house and business to that unexpected tragedy the worst thing that ever happened to you? Was it even a bad thing, or was it truly a blessing in disguise? Think about it. I know that I have, because you're reading the book that resulted from that series of events.

When things look their worst to us is when we're receiving some of the best direction we'll ever get. Sometimes we need to be humbled to quiet the noise inside and hear Spirit calling. I was on the wrong path. Did I go through a lot to change paths? You bet I did, but the adjustment pains and the time it required were only in proportion to my resistance to the changes that life was presenting to me. As soon as I learned to use the flow concept, it suddenly got much easier. So, you see, writing a thank-you letter every night for all that has happened to you that day, especially the negative things, is very important. Some of the things we first perceive as the worst things that have ever happened have created the most wonderful aspects and opportunities in our lives. Don't be quick to judge, but be very quick to be grateful.

You may ask, "Why do I have to write this on paper and force myself to be grateful when there are some days I'm just not feeling very grateful?" Acknowledge that you don't feel grateful, but then go through the motions. It's a discipline that will work wonders for you if you employ it. It doesn't require your permission to work, just your actions.

Back in the day, long before most of us probably remember, gratitude was usually referred to *a debt of gratitude*. Gratitude is a sort of debt in that we are on the receiving end of someone else's generous action, for which we did nothing in exchange. We understand that there is usually a reciprocating half to any exhange, which leaves us feeling that we should do something for the other person, that we owe them somehow. This concept establishes gratitude as an action. Let me explain. Your friend gives you a wonderful crystal vase as a gift. The vase is absolutely breathtaking. You're overwhelmed with gratitude for it and can't thank them enough (gratitude and thanks are not the same thing). You display it as a centerpiece so that others can see this wonderful gift and you make sure to dust it off frequently so that it's always seen as the beautiful piece that it is. Your actions are speaking gratitude every time your friend comes over, sees it sitting there clean and beautiful for all to see. Her heart is warmed because she knows she's brought joy to your life. The next time your birthday or a holiday comes around, what kind of gift do you think she'll give you? I bet she'll select something else that's beautiful and wonderful, because it will have been inspired by the action of the gratitude that she saw you demonstrate with the crystal vase. It made her feel good inside knowing you received it with the same care and love with which she gave it.

Now, on the other hand, say you give someone a really nice set of china. You take the time to select a wonderful pattern on the most beautiful china you can find. You go to their house for dinner several times, yet you never see them use the china. It's not even displayed in their hutch and it appears that they could care less. There's no sense of gratitude past the smile and thank you that they gave you when they opened it. What do you think you'll get them next time? If they aren't your children, your heart most likely won't be in it.

Once again, gratitude is an action, not necessarily a feeling, although feelings can be present. This is why you write it down and discipline yourself to take these gratitude actions. The feelings and attitude of gratitude will follow later.

This exercise has yielded more results for more people then you can imagine. Gratitude expressed as I have described it is a karmic proposition. In other words, like begets like. If you put out good energy regarding the things in your life, you'll naturally attract more good things to you in a positive way. In the realm of gratitude, we're dealing with complete and total abundance in its purest form. You cannot attract more if you're only grateful for what you have, but you can be grateful for what others have, creating an even greater attraction point for yourself, while helping them energetically. There is never a shortage. No one really takes from the other.

There's always more than enough to go around when you deal in the realm of gratitude. Gratitude is like a magnet. The more you have, the more you attract; the more grateful you are for what you don't see in your life yet, the more rapidly the space opens up for it to manifest in your life. If you want to consciously manifest things in your life, don't just visualize yourself having it and act as if it is already in your life—become grateful for it *already being* in your life. The energy of gratitude will create the space for your desired outcome and act like a magnet, bringing it to you with great momentum. It increases the flow of your desire towards you by putting to work the physics formula of momentum: Momentum = Mass × Speed × Direction.

When you become truly grateful for something in your life, even if it isn't there yet, it generates emotion and deep feeling. When emotion gets behind your desire and intent, the results are phenomenal. Gratitude pulls all of the forces of nature together, with the elements of flow creating your deepest desires. I once learned about a process called *Be, Do, Have*, which is the natural order of creation. In our society, we're trained to go against the natural order of things. Maybe this is why we have so many problems with nature and the environment, as well as relationships. We believe that we must first *have* something in order to *do* what people that *have* that item *do*, so we can *be* someone or something. However, the natural order of things is to first *be* who or what you want to *be*, and then that will lead to you *doing* the things that people who are already in that frame of being *do* and you will *have* what they *have*, and beyond.

Let me give you an example. Most people believe that if they *have* the right job making the right money, they can buy (*do*) a really nice home in a great neighborhood and they will *be* happy. They struggle for years beating their heads against the wall, working and stressed out all the time, destroying themselves and their family to achieve this goal so they can be happy. Many never even reach it, but leave behind a path of destruction. How can this be a natural order of things when you really look and analyze it? It can't, and it's not. Creation, not destruction, is the natural order of things. The natural way is to first *be* happy within and then *do* the things that people who are happy *do*, and you will *have* what happy people *have* without all the stress. If you believe happy people have great jobs making good money with nice houses in a wonderful neighborhood to raise their families, then that's what you'll have, without all the struggle.

Gratitude lifts and enlivens us, relieving the burden from our backs. It creates tremendous energy within us and acts as our conscious statement of genuine humility. When a person is grateful, they're giving thanks to a greater force at work. They are not acting as the alpha and omega. They are acknowledging that something else is at work in their life. They become free of many of the things that drain them every day.

I once undertook a 40-day fast and discovered a number of things about myself. The most significant thing that I learned is that food does not provide our energy—it gives us strength and stamina. Energy is something we receive from the thoughts we hold. I went through the gratitude process, making it a functional part of my day and became more in touch with all of the good and wonderful things in my life. I purged my negative thoughts using thoughts of gratitude whenever anything negative would come up. At the end of the fasting, I had only lost 14 pounds, but had never had so much energy in my life. I felt great and alive, at a level I hadn't experienced since childhood, if then. On the 38th day, a significantly negative situation occurred, but instead of panicking and buying into it, I became grateful for the situation and what I would learn from it. Needless to say, after a couple of weeks, the problem faded and my life continued in a wonderful way. When I started eating again, I kept the gratitude process in my life, and though I have modified it to some degree and I'm not so rigid with it as I once was, it still amazes me to see it at work.

Remember this: gratitude is the cement that bonds together all the elements in the dynamic laws of creation and the Art of Flow. If you're truly grateful, you won't be in your own way any longer. Self-centeredness cannot live in the same environment as an attitude of gratitude. Once you become grateful and take action on it, everything else will flow to you naturally, so be grateful for all that you have, all that you have had, and all that you will have in the future on this, your great journey of life.

EXERCISE GRATITUDE

Purchase a separate notebook and call it your gratitude journal. Put it next to your bed. Every morning before your feet hit the floor, grab your notebook and on a right-hand-facing page, make a random list of all the things you have to be grateful for that day, especially the people in your life and the things that you have planned for that day. Give thanks that everything will work out in a way that will serve you to the highest good and the ideas you have of yourself. Give thanks with a feeling of tremendous gratitude for them.

That evening just before you retire, write a thank-you letter on the left-facing page. Give thanks for all the wonderful things about that day. When you get to the end of the letter, be sure you write a special thank-you for all of the things that didn't work out or that you perceived as bad or negative in that day. Be sure to include those people who may have angered you or upset or hurt you in any way. Give thanks with deep gratitude for these people, events, situations and conditions. Be clear about the idea that you are grateful for them, even though you do not yet know or comprehend how they will serve you to your highest good. This is the most important part of this letter.

If you do this for 30 days, at the end of that time you'll notice many subtle, positive changes in your life. You will find that you are truly grateful for everything—whether you personally perceive it as good or bad, positive or negative. You will find it is easier to accept things in life that come at you and accept people for who they are.

OPEN-MINDEDNESS

- chapter fifteen -

As long as you're convinced that you know, you will never know. When you begin to comprehend that you don't know, you start to know a little.

To be in a state of open-mindedness requires humility and an absence of judgment. It is to be without a fixed idea of how things are or how they're supposed to be, according to your personal designs and preferences. It is living in a state of not knowing, or as we've mentioned throughout this text, "no mind." To be open-minded is to acknowledge that you do not have the answers or know how things are really supposed to be. It is to step beyond pride and ego and realize the concept that, *The more you learn, the less you really know.*

Being in this state of mind runs parallel with living a life based in trust and faith. It means that a person living in this state isn't running around with some God complex or power trip. They are fluid and at choice, and this is the power behind open-mindedness. When we're fluid and at choice, it means that we're in the moment and deciding on our options and actions using information currently in front of us, instead of some past pattern or belief.

Open-mindedness allows for the ultimate level of creation. When someone is open to all possible results instead of fixed on a specific result, they can set forth intent, with results following quickly. They aren't locking into place their ideas of what it should look like, and are instead just holding a space for their intent to show up. Open-mindedness is the ultimate mindset of space because it has no limitation or resistance at any level; it is receptive and fertile, like that of the female body at the point just prior to conception. It is a vessel of limitless possibility.

In my research on the life of Jesus, what I learned was that there was no one that he excluded and no one he didn't accept—even at the criticism of his own followers. He knew that some of the most loyal of his people would be ones who had violated the laws of humanity and spirit but were accepted in spite of that. He held his door open wide for all to enter, even to those who did not want it right away. He could only have done this by not passing judgment on them. His way was all-inclusive, never exclusive.

There have been many times in my life when I've had someone who wronged me later come to my door and reach out a hand for help. It was in reaching back to these individuals that I experienced some of my greatest growth and learning. These moments have been instrumental in forging who I am today. Many times, I found that I was equally responsible for some aspect of what had happened between us. In this way, I found forgiveness and self-acceptance. I would like to share a brief experience with you.

My ex-wife and her husband had been living in New Orleans when Hurricane Katrina hit. Needless to say, they suffered great losses and had nowhere to go. Knowing my sons were watching, I had to make a decision. It only took a moment, but I decided to offer them a hand and put everything that had transpired behind me. I wish I could say it was easy, but it made me confront myself and my own rigid point of view. She had left me and moved in with him, breaking up the family and generating some serious resentments and anger within me. Even though I was past those feelings, I still had a very limited of viewpoint where they were concerned. Somewhere deep inside, some victim/perpetrator conversations were still lodged in place. Reaching out to help them and allowing them to stay with us off and on while they repaired their home to sell it gave me the opportunity to confront myself in a new way, which led to greater openness and acceptance of myself at a deeper level. It was quite revealing and enlightening.

In the very beginning, I saw the whole thing as somewhat of an inconvenience, but I've become very grateful for the whole experience and what the outcome has been. It granted me a greater understanding of who and what I am as a person; it revealed some deep issues I might not have otherwise seen and overcome; it empowered me to a greater level of love and self-acceptance; and it gave me freedom on a number of levels. One was because they moved to the city in which I live and for a time shared in some of the responsibilities for my youngest son; and second, because I found freedom in letting go of the last victim/perpetrator conversations I had regarding that situation. Lastly, the experience also expanded my ability to be more open-minded and forgiving, leaving me with lasting growth. Looking back, I came out on top.

When they moved back to New Orleans several years later, it was really quite a disruption. All of us, as one big modern family unit, were used to doing everything together. Though I still occasionally had personality conflicts with my former wife, as I guess anyone could expect, she and her husband had become a working, active part of the family, and it was very nice. The prejudices I once held, whether justified or not, were gone. In my heart I only had love for them and the wonderful benefits we received from them actively being part of the family. I know my sons and grandchildren miss those close family interactions that were only made possible by the open-mindedness created from a disaster the size of Hurricane Katrina.

When I look closely, all of the greatest events in my life were first surrounded by a mindset of open-mindedness. Unfortunately, it usually required some great event or disaster to get me to open up, but it had to happen before the good in my life could flow in. This was all before I really embraced these essential principles of flow. An open mind is like a clean, white canvas, receptive and waiting for the artist. When the mind is not open, it's like trying to create a new painting on top of one that's already there, working around something that distracts and gets in the way of creativity. Before replacing what's there, it's much better to coat it with primer and make the canvas a clean, blank slate again.

Over time, much of the work I do with others has simplified tremendously. I see it all so easily that I often tell others that if you want to be in the Flow, simply move out of the way. This is usually too simple for them, because they can't understand how to move out of the way. This chapter gives me a chance to clear that up. The only factor preventing you or I from having the life that we truly desire is ourselves. Therefore, to move out of the way is to simply clear out the fixed beliefs, ideas, stories, and judgments in our minds in order to create a space of humility (state of being teachable). By doing this, we create a state of open-mindedness which will never fail to serve us to our highest good and the highest good of everyone around us.

EXERCISE OPEN-MINDEDNESS

Open-mindedness begins when we are willing to release our judgments and beliefs on a given area or topic in our lives. See if you can list five areas of difficulty in your life right now. For each one, write down your specific beliefs about it, especially the things you are a position about.

After you've done this, reflect on how your beliefs, judgments and positions might be affecting these areas of difficulty. See if you can understand how, if you released these beliefs and positions, it might facilitate a quicker outcome. Once you have reflected on this for a short while, pull out a pen and paper and write for about five minutes using the following guide statements.

I hold on to my _____ belief, judgment, or position regarding _____ because . . .

Or,

I hold on to my beliefs about _____ regarding _____ because . . .

When you're finished, disregard the first minute and the last minute of your writing and pay close attention what you wrote during the middle three minutes. Fair warning, you might discover the real reason you hang on to these limitations that are holding you back and creating pain and suffering. The true, underlying reason you're holding on so tightly could be because you're afraid of what might happen if you don't control the result, or that you may not get the outcome you desire. Maybe you should try a new strategy!

Set an intention out in the Universe for your desired result to come to fruition, write it down, and then walk away from it. Don't think of it anymore. Release it to Spirit and let it fly, trusting that it will be delivered in the best way for the greater good of you and everyone involved. Don't reflect on it or determine how you would like it to manifest. See if by letting go it comes to you quickly or if the opportunity for it to manifest does not present itself faster in your life than if you had tried to control the result or held a vision of how it should look.

When you release how it should look, you're creating the space and giving permission to the Universe to create your intention on its own terms.

TRUTH

- chapter sixteen -

The truth will set you free.

I'm sure we have all heard the saying "the truth will set you free", over and over again. So, what is it about this phrase that makes it so powerful? When you think about it, what are they really talking about? Truth can have so many meanings! Are they equating truth with honesty, or referencing the laws of physics? Are they referring to universal truths (like the Laws of Attraction) or personal truths, as in what is true for you and me personally? What *is* the truth? What makes it the truth? How do we know it *is* the truth? Isn't the truth a continually changing concept for each individual?

If this is the line of questioning that comes into your mind when you ponder the idea of truth, then you're definitely headed in the right direction. When Jesus told parables and made statements, he told them in such a way that they continually unfurl new layers as each of matures in our comprehension of life and spirit. In other words, what is the truth for you today? If you continue to grow spiritually on a daily basis, the things that are a constant for you now won't necessarily be truths for you a month or a year from now. The power in the concept of truth will be continually revealing itself to you as you become ready to see it.

In this book, I don't seek to feed you answers, but to intrigue your mind and stimulate questions so that you might find what is true for yourself. The truth lives in the question, not in the answer. Once the answer has been received, its power is lost and the energy of the question is gone. It's been fulfilled, like a flower that reaches full bloom and begins to perish. Birth requires receptivity, and for each answer to be found there must first be the birth of a question—a vessel of receptivity that will lead you to the truth as it is right for you. No two people are ever stimulated by the same set of questions. The truth must first have a space to be born into—a space to receive it—and a mind that is open and acknowledges that it does not "know." Therefore, the truth can only be unveiled to a degree equal to the question and to the space of the vessel that has been prepared to receive the answer.

When we begin this life, we only know truth; we're an empty page of receptivity waiting for the truth of life to be unveiled to us. Then, as we begin to grow, we're given input that becomes our truth. In most cases, the input is riddled with errors and problems, but nevertheless becomes what is true for us. As we get older, we relearn about truth in the area of honesty. As funny as it may seem, we came into the world empty and in complete truth, but by the time we're 5 or 6, we're being re-taught what we already knew, though in a way that conforms more to the community consciousness. Try making sense of that.

As children, we're taught truth in the sense of honesty, while being stripped of our personal truth in favor of what others believe, such as our parents, teachers and the community. As teenagers, our personal level of truth becomes a very elusive, changeable concept depending on what our motives are. Usually, we begin to interpret truth selectively, based on our desires. We call this manipulation . . . maybe you've heard of it? Teenagers are masters at it, especially with their parents. If you ask a teenager about the concept of honesty/truth and how they apply it in their lives, more often than not you'll notice a small smile and that they look away or completely resist the conversation, as if you were attacking them. Manipulation, lying, and selective interpretation of the truth are a few of the primary ontological distinctions of adolescence.

As we enter early adulthood, we begin to look for our place in life. Unfortunately, we've usually lost ourselves by then, buried under tons of crap and inaccuracies that we've learned. These very things have become *a* truth for us (our identity, in some cases) but not *the* truth. The process is that of uncovering ourselves, layer-by-layer. The more we scrape back the layers of beliefs and judgments, casting aside the stories we live in, the higher the quality of life we find inside. The more closely we listen in silence, the louder the truth becomes. These are personal truths — what is true for you individually, as well as who you really are deep inside — your connection to Oneness. Once released, this is the part of us that brings us in complete alignment to life, and it begins to serve us. This is being in the Flow. Strange as it may be, when brought into the light of truth, a seemingly hopeless situation can be turned around in order to have an abundant and beautiful life. Even an empty life filled with material wealth can become transformed into a full life filled with love and generosity. Whatever your station and situation, life can suddenly turn around so that what once seemed impossible will become the norm.

Of course, as this happens, truth will include impeccable honesty—the acknowledgment of universal truths and our own personal truths. It will all fold into itself as one and become *the* truth, *our* truth and the *only* truth . . . for us. This truth makes each of us completely unique, because we all have something a little different to contribute to life. We will always know the truth because the truth will always stand up. It will never fail or falter. Truth is the truth today, tomorrow, next week, and next year. Know that the truth *is* and will always be. Trust it, question it (open-mindedly), and it will never fail you. All you have to do is move aside and let it grow within you. It will, in fact, set you free.

EXERCISE TRUTH

See if you can find five things that you believed were the absolute truth when you were young and write them down. Track the changes of that truth through your current age. Many times we find that a single idea or truth will change about every seven to 10 years. With that in mind, start with concepts you had as a child, then when you were a teenager, and then keep progressing in increments of 10 years until you reach your current age. Investigate how you were changed through programming, new information, or experiences that led you to your present ideas of what the truth is for you.

In my own life, I used to get into discussions or arguments and believed that I was constantly in the right. I was very smart and was often factually correct about some things. However, as I grew up I began to notice that other elements factored into each situation. I suddenly realized that I wasn't right back then, but now that I had all the answers I was convinced that *this* time I knew what I was talking about. A number of years would pass, then I'd begin to notice that I wasn't so right about any of that, either. It finally occurred to me that there were no absolute answers and that it is a person's perception of the actual topic being discussed that affected whether or not anything was "correct".

Because I was always basing things on my own experiences and interpretations and factoring out the other person's, I realized I couldn't be right about anything outside of my own stockpile of information on a topic. Even if I use the term *"I know,"* nowadays, you can bet that in the back of my mind, I am aware and realizing that I'm merely speculating, based on the combination of my experience and what I'm hearing you say. Not bad for a guy who would have argued you to the grave on any given topic. This also taught me that I could choose happiness over being right all the time, which I would definitely say is a nice byproduct of the process.

SELF-SABOTAGE AND FAILURE

- chapter seventeen -

There is no such thing as failure—only results.

When I was younger, I thought I was walking around with a big "X" on my back because nothing I did seemed to work out in the long term. In fact, everything in my life seemed to be like a short-run, off-Broadway play. It opened with a bang, continued for a short while, and then saw a final curtain. I thought I was a defect of some kind and actually began to believe it. Like many, I had grown resigned to "my station" in life, believing that I was destined to being a chronic failure.

One day, I realized that I was responsible for a lot of my failures and had actually done things that sabotaged my relationships and certain ventures I would undertake. When I stumbled across this information and began to really get it, I figured that if I was open, learned my lessons, and released certain issues in life, I would finally get what I wanted. Much to my surprise, the more that I believed this, the more success I achieved.

Even though things were going well, I always seemed to be limited to a certain level of success. I would assess each situation and conclude that there had to be something I didn't completely understand; there were things I was supposed to learn or overcome. I would proceed to harshly judge and analyze myself and events, looking for the smallest details that I might need to work on or overcome, diligently searching for those little imperfections in my character that I missed and needed to assassinate in order to be successful.

You might be thinking that I was being too tough on myself, but if you had known me then, you wouldn't think so. I was ruthless when it came to trying to uncover these things, and even made a personal inventory of my character and my behaviors at one point. I asked a good friend if he would discuss it with me. He was a tremendous coach and had a background in doing this kind of thing, yet when we sat down and spoke he became overwhelmed by the results of my self-analysis and needed to take a break to process the information and get a grip on it. He was blown away by how deep and gritty some of it was, and explained to me that I had gone to a depth way beyond the point where anyone should be analyzing themselves. He thought it must have been incredibly brutal—much more brutal than it needed to be. There were others around that time that were also telling me to be gentle with myself, but I just didn't get it. I refused to leave any stone unturned.

A number of years later, I went through Life Mastery Training with Alan Cohen in Maui and realized I had brutalized myself, and that I had done it all as a means of moving things out of the way in order to achieve success in life. I just thought it was how I was supposed to do things. Alan taught me that I could do the same thing with gentleness and allow Spirit to work through me and with me. Without knowing it, Alan taught me the meaning of space as far as it applied to transformational work, as well as how it applied to my own transformation. For that week, he held a space where transformation could take place and taught us just to honor ourselves. The experience was extremely powerful, and I recommend it to anyone.

It's like a scenario a friend of mine uses in one of his talks to illustrate growth: "A doctor does not heal—he creates an aseptic environment in which healing can take place and Spirit does the healing. A farmer does not grow—he creates a fertile environment where growth can take place and Spirit does the growing. We cannot change; we can create an environment in which change can take place and Spirit does the changing."

This is a profound and fantastic truth. We merely hold a space in which manifestation, transformation, and change can occur, and the Universe/Spirit/God, or whatever you prefer to reference, does the manifestation, creation, and changing.

If all of this is true, then we can't possibly fail at anything. We make a decision and accompanying action, and what we get are results—not success or failure. Failure is a *judgment* set in motion by some belief that we have. It is not truth. It is based on programming and an idea that we developed or were given very early in life as to what would constitute success. In my case, I couldn't ever succeed. When I was young, I learned a standard of success that had me comparing myself against a measuring stick that would lengthen itself as I got closer to the top. In other words, the degree by which I measured success kept changing. No matter what I did, it was never enough. In this way, I was always doomed to fail. I was told as a child that I would never amount to much in life, and I made sure that happened by changing the measure of success that I applied.

Eventually, I would give up—validating my belief that I would never stack up against what my father thought I should be.

My life was altered forever the day I realized that there was no right or wrong, no good or bad, no failure or success. All of them are merely judgments based on perceptions rooted in my belief system. This may not sound like much, but it was an electric feeling and gave me a sensation of freedom. I finally saw that these were the chains binding me to the tracks, waiting for a train that would inevitably hit me and make me its victim every time.

At this point you might be wondering: If there's no such thing as failure, then why do I sabotage myself?

The answer is quite simple. We sabotage ourselves so that we won't measure up and will continue to validate the beliefs that we have. Not an easy prospect to come to terms with, but it is a large part of self-sabotage. There is, however, an entirely different reason I've learned and would like to share with you.

It goes like this. When I was young, I had a sense of where I was going in life, but never really adhered to it. When I was 10, I overheard a nun remark to my mother that I would become a writer. By the age of 15, I was being encouraged by medical staff at a hospital to write a book about the near-death experience I had when I died in their ER following a tragic accident. When I came back around, all I knew was that I had some questions about what I saw and finally worked up the nerve to ask. I told them specific details of the experience and what I remembered about it. These were details I could only know if I had actually witnessed what took place in the room after I flat-lined. I absolutely refused to write the book because I figured that people would think I was some sort of freak. (This was years before anyone felt comfortable talking to the public or media about this stuff.)

Although I had notebooks full of ideas and writing projects, I continued to move toward other activities that seemed much more exciting to me, many of which involved making a great deal of money. In school, I was a very bad student and always behind. I would cut a deal with the teachers to write a special paper for them if they would just give me the grade I needed in order to pass to the next level. By 24, I had written my first full-length screenplay. At the age of 29, I was a hired gun for college students, helping them write their papers in a variety of subject areas, as well as coaching some of them on writing. Several times in my 30s, I attempted to pick it up again, but never stuck with it, and then in my 40s, I became the publisher of a magazine for which I had to compose a publisher's letter each month. Today, I am writing seriously and with dedication, and have never felt better.

If you're asking what this has to do with self-sabotage, let me explain. The truth for me is that life was trying to guide me down a road of coaching and writing for many, many years. I would do the coaching because it made me feel good about myself, but I didn't get the same immediate gratification from the writing. It simply took longer and the payoff was delayed. My opinion is that the flow of life kept trying to lift me up into my bliss and I kept resisting it. I would try all these different paths, looking for that inner satisfaction and fulfillment, and though I would find success for a while, they would inevitably dead-end. I believe today that what I term "self-sabotage" is nothing more than my inner self attempting to direct me down the path I was put here to travel.

I believe that we all subconsciously know what we're supposed to do, but we have to follow our internal guidance to get there. This is important. Even though I spent years trying other things, coaching and writing are what I truly love and are where I've always gotten the greatest personal reward. It enlivens and energizes me to help others. I wasn't able to see this until I became the publisher of Natural Awakenings magazine in Northeast Florida and had to write for the public every month. I would also say this is probably why I have been successful as long as I have as a publisher.

Someone asked me whether I thought it was even necessary for me to go down all those paths to gain the experience I needed for coaching. While I concede that's a good point, I don't think it's really a consideration, because it simply wasn't an option. I resisted that path and tried others because I knew subconsciously that I wasn't ready to be a writer and workshop facilitator. Besides, I always thought success was about making more money. I wouldn't trade those valuable experiences for anything, however misguided they seem today. I do believe that if I'd felt ready and wanted to go down the road to being a facilitator and writer earlier, everything would have been fine and I would have had just as much to offer as I do now.

I want to reiterate that there is no such thing as failure. Failure is merely a judgment that we make, and is based on some personal belief of how things should be. If failure is only a judgment, then there can be no self-sabotage—only redirection from a higher guidance. You could liken it to those little robot vacuum cleaners that roam around the house; when they bump into a surface, they just turn and redirect themselves onto a new path. The difference between you and that little robot is that it doesn't have a personal investment in making any specific direction work—it doesn't resist changing course. If we did the same, life would simply flow to us, almost effortlessly. Remember—the pains that you experience in life (speaking mentally and emotionally) are in exact proportion to your resistance to change or changing course. We need these corrections to find our true path in life.

Don't go through life thinking like I did, that you're broken or that you're marked for failure. Realize the truth in nature and know that you are perfect just as you are, where you are. The worst thing I ever did was judging who and what I was so harshly. I stood in constant judgment of the things I did and thought poorly of myself because they didn't measure up to what I thought I was supposed to be. I would look around, judging my insides against everyone else's outsides, and it just didn't seem as if I was a very good person. Accept yourself as you are—the authentic you that resides inside—and you will truly be able to make the judgment that you are a success. This is what I've learned to do and the world is a happier place for me.

Keep in mind that the more harshly you judge yourself, the more harshly you will judge others. If you seek to be less judgmental in life, start with yourself. Be gentle and loving, and know that if you've made it through the day, you're already a success . . . really, everyone is. See the love and success in yourself and you will see it in others. On the flip side of things, if you *can* see the love and success in others, it's because it's reflecting back the wondrous qualities of success within you—all you have to do is tap into those qualities by not judging and condemning yourself.

EXERCISE RELEASING YOUR MEASURING STICK

Reflect on a time when you were just about to get to the pinnacle of a project or goal you were achieving, but things suddenly didn't work out, or maybe you did achieve it and things began to fall apart shortly after.

How were you measuring your success? Did you consider yourself a failure for what you had lost or a success for the degree of your achievement? When was the last time you achieved something most people would consider a success, but you got down on yourself because you didn't feel like you had actually achieved a high enough level? Were you moving the measuring stick to keep yourself from feeling successful?

Now go back and reflect on those achievements and accomplishments again, but this time, imagine how things might have been better if you had just viewed them as a success or not judged them at all. What would your life have been like? What would your life be like today? Imagine the sweetness of it all.

Realize right now that the way you view these things can be reset. You can crush the measuring stick, release your judgments, and see these things as they really were—activities that taught you lessons and led you to new and greater activities. See yourself as a winner, because you continued to move forward from one experience to the next in life. You are a success, because you care enough about the quality of your life to keep growing and learning, including finding books like this one to study. See yourself as a dynamic experience of complete perfection in every way, because everything you have done and everything that you do will always serve the greater good for you and everyone around you. Go ahead right now and forgive yourself for seeing it the old way; reframe each event in your life as an experience of success in a life filled with success and love every day. By simply forgiving yourself and reframing all the events in your life, you will smash the measuring stick once and for all. You will be free.

HUMILITY

- chapter eighteen -

The Key to All Transformation

Humility is the key that unlocks the door to all transformation. At first glance, you might wonder how a word we rarely hear in everday conversation and know so little about be so important. As I muddled around in search of my own transformation, I discovered that this little word had tremendous meaning and many applications, yet they were all the same when I broke them down. It brought me to the conclusion that the simplest definition of humility is nothing more than a state of being teachable.

To be teachable, we must first realize that we don't have all the answers. That's step one—"I don't know." The second is that when we realize that we don't know, there should be a quieting or reduction of the ego and how much it manipulates us. In this space, we're able to be present in the moment. Suddenly, our little thoughts and schemes do not dominate us. Almost everyone resists being in this favorable mental state, yet it is in this mind—the mindset of *no mind*—that we begin to embrace *being*, at which point enlightenment may find us.

But what does it mean to be humble and how does it look? How does it affect us and why should we seek what appears to be such a powerless state of mind?

Essentially, the state of humility is a state of strength and grace. It is a place where we can allow the flow of life to move through us and shift us into our natural directions, where we fit perfectly and are of the most benefit to ourselves and to the rest of the world. It is the space where we break the race consciousness or community consciousness and begin to experience and follow our own inner voice. In this way, we can never fail; we merely flow into the experiences that are necessary and perfect for us in any given moment.

The power of humility is the power of *being,* and that means that we are completely "in choice"" in any given moment. The only real power any of us have on this Earth is the power of choice. You might hear many women make statements like, "I've taken my power back," or "I've reclaimed my power." I find it very interesting that when I ask them what exactly is this power that they've reclaimed, almost none of them have ever been able to nail down what it is. They may not be able to identify or describe it, but they feel it deep within. Finally, after asking this numerous times, one lady finally told me she took back her power of choice in life. I was floored. I had asked this over and over again and finally someone got it. I acknowledged her understanding and explained that she was absolutely on target. It was a moment of beauty for both of us.

It's not just women who give their power away. Unfortunately, we all do—all genders alike. For instance, a lot of women can't see how it would apply to men, but it does. Imagine you were raised to be a certain way by your parents and the community at large, told that you had to be the provider, the protector, and the pillar of strength at all times for the family unit. You're told that you're supposed to be able to go out and kill your dinner and be the king in your castle, or that all life should center around the male when he comes home. Sounds far-fetched to you? Just look around, because most baby boomers were raised in a very similar fashion. They were programmed from the day they were born for all of the above. In this way, they have no real choice in life. It's the same way that so many girls are programmed, but for them, it is to give away their power to the male.

Because of this cultural mindset, none of us have choice until we take it back. To do so usually requires an enormous force that lands us on the rocks. That moment of pain and despair when we feel we cannot go one step further is when humility sets in and we realize we don't have the answers—we just give up! It is usually marked by a cry for help. That's the moment in which we regain choice. It is the most powerful personal human experience we will ever have. It is the greatest oxymoron we will ever witness—to give up our power through defeat and yet gain more power than we've ever known—all through the experience of giving up complete control. This is true power, and one of mankind's greatest paradoxes of truth. When we finally let go and give up, we begin to break away from our current mindset and do some things differently. We suddenly find ourselves making choices we normally wouldn't have made, first in desperation and then because we see them working.

When I realize that I am not the center of the Universe, I begin to grow and flow in a natural direction. However, it requires great sacrifice and detachment. It requires the elimination of our best friend—our ego. To do this often does take losing nearly everything or having some life-altering experience. Many years ago, I battled with alcohol and smoking dope. It was a tremendous crutch for me growing up because I had to endure a significant amount of abuse in my life, and at one point it medicated me in a way that I needed in order to survive. The day came, however, when it became my reason for living; I landed on the rocks, where I crashed and burned. Some friends were there to provide a little help, and one in particular taught me a lesson in humility I will never forget. My friend was probably 10 to 15 years older than me, and his nickname was Hollywood.

I had taken all the information that my friends had given me and set out to do life without drinking, although I have to admit that I never really saw a problem with pot. It mellowed me out and helped chill my volatile temper. I would run into Hollywood occasionally and he would ask how things were going, knowing I had put down the drink but still smoked weed. Each time he asked how I was doing, I would smile and say I was doing fine. Each time, as if he'd rehearsed it, he would say, "You ain't gonna make it."

I was shopping for a car one day in the dealership showroom where he worked and we went through the routine again. I didn't understand why he would constantly repeat this same statement and I was so frustrated that I grabbed the lapels on his jacket and shook him and said, "What, are you blind? Can't you see I am making it and doing fine . . . what is your problem?" When I released him, he straightened his jacket, smiled and said, "You ain't gonna make it." I stormed out of there.

Fast-forward a number of months. I went to the hospital because of some breathing issues, and the doctors informed me that I had the early stages of emphysema. I was told I had to stop smoking whatever I was smoking or I wouldn't survive much longer. On the way home I cried, realizing I couldn't stop smoking and deal with the normal functions of life. A week later, I was on my way to ending my life, but instead ended up with my friends. I showed up at our little club that day, completely defeated, depressed, and not knowing how I would make it—and there was Hollywood, spinning around on a parking meter talking to a few friends. When he saw me, he proceeded to go through the routine, except when he asked how I was doing I replied, "I'm not going to make it." He stopped in his tracks, stepped toward me, and put his finger in my face. With a huge smile he said, "*Now* you're going to make it." Frustrated and defeated, I asked, "What do you mean? I can't handle this!" He looked at me very caringly and said, "As long as you know—you'll never know, and when you begin to know that you don't know, then you start to know a little, because the "We" can always do what the "I" can't."

Now, as foggy as I was, as humbled as I was, I was still able to wrap my mind around that concept. I realized that I had become an island unto myself and he had seen me as a sinking ship the whole time. He knew that the longer I used, the more I was separating myself, becoming so isolated from help that it would eventually take me down. He just waited for me with a life raft. I would later learn for myself how much discipline that took on his part. Another side of it is that I later realized that the more we learn, the less we know, and that until we experience a true level of humility, we cannot truly embrace a state of grace, even though it's all around us.

Needless to say, I was able to put down smoking dope. I owe my lesson in understanding the importance of humility to Hollywood: "Unto myself, I am nothing; belief in separation is false and just doesn't work . . . at least not for me." Humility creates a state of grace in which change can and does take place, if we allow it. It is the highest state for learning.

EXERCISE HUMILITY

Consider all of the ways that you separate yourself from others in your life and your experiences, and then consider all of the ways you're connected to others. Do you find that you have a clearer, much better experience when you're connected to others? If you're like many people, you won't, and that's O.K.

Either way, write down a list of what you believe to be your greatest solo accomplishments. Next, let's reconsider just how solo they really were. Let's say you got a big promotion for the work you did on a project because it made the company a great deal of money or saved them a great deal of money. All the accolades went to you, and rightly so, because you are the one that did the research and stayed up late at night building those studies and creating those reports. Congratulations.

Now take each one of those accomplishments that you did by yourself and let's take a different look at them. Didn't someone bring you into the world and raise you, helping you get an education and giving you funding and guidance? No? O.K, so you were an orphan who worked full-time, went to school, and applied for grants. No problem. The orphanage and people that ran and funded it saw to your daily needs. The teachers, the students in your classes, and all of the millions of people who paid for your very public education need to be considered. Then there is the person who hired you for the job that kept you alive during college, giving you experience that ultimately led to your current job. Don't forget the HR staff that supported you, not to mention your coworkers or your bosses, to list a few more. And of course, there are the people that invented all those wonderful tools you used to create the packages and do the research, everyone who contributed to creating the Internet, and oh, yeah, the people who paid for you to have these wonderful machines and tools to use.

By now I am sure you get my point here that you can't do anything alone. Not really. Everything we do is connected to many other people in some way, shape, or form, including the clothes you wore to get the job and get the promotion. We don't work alone—it's just not how things are.

Now make a list of all of the people with each of those accomplishments that supported you in any and every way you can imagine to create that new job opportunity and promotion, or in your case, whatever achievements you listed. Recognize the number of people involved in your success every day. Once you truly embrace this, you'll begin to feel a little smaller (realizing how many people are involved in your life) and a little larger (being part of something much larger than yourself) all at once, but without the ego. You'll realize how blessed you are to have such wonderful support and begin to feel a new level of humility. You'll become a little more teachable, a little more vulnerable, and a little more humble because you realize there is more to the world than just you.

DENIED ASPECTS OF SELF

- chapter nineteen -

*If a tree fell in the woods and everyone was there to hear it,
would anyone claim it?*

Almost all of us have certain very real, intangible aspects of ourselves that we deny. These aspects of ourselves are very important points of power that affect every single element of our make-up. It's not really something that's easy for us to see, but it is incredibly obvious to others. Often, it may be a very strong quality in us that's very present in everything we do, and yet we go through life denying that we have it. Other times, it isn't as obvious in our actions but it creates the tone in which the actions are done.

For instance, I denied my own worthiness. For years, I felt completely unworthy of anything good in my life, and I'm sure that it stemmed from the fact that I was adopted, felt like a throwaway, and that my father (adoptive, of course) constantly told me how worthless and horrible I was as a teenager and how I would amount to nothing. You see, the things that I believed were valuable were things for which he had zero appreciation or interest. That made me worthless to him. One day, I took a workshop that focused on the very elements of ourselves that we deny, and I came out a new man. I walked taller, had a bigger smile, and felt like I belonged here on this planet for once.

Declaring the existence of these elements of yourself that you've denied most of your life is a very powerful experience. It is just that simple—finding, locating, and declaring ownership of that aspect of Self. For most people, it has to do with love, beauty, worthiness, gender, and the like. The list can be quite long, but generally sorts itself out under five or ten different headings that can manifest in a hundred different ways, making each person very unique in how they show up.

So how do you know which aspects of yourself are being stymied and what to do about it? This is where a group or support framework comes in very handy and can help you accomplish these things. In the absence of a great workshop or support group, you can begin to observe yourself and ask people around you how they see you. If you choose the latter method, be prepared, because this can be a very painful process; most people have no idea of how the world truly views them. In my opinion, a workshop is the best way to achieve this result because (as is the standard in my own workshops) there is an experienced facilitator and a staff who are very seasoned and can make this a very gentle process. In addition, you are participating with individuals who only know you in a workshop format for a short time and are willing to be gut-level honest with you—for your benefit, as well as their own. Ever notice how easy it is to be the most honest with people you really don't know? This can be extremely useful for situations like this.

Let's say that you've tried asking the people around you and in the process have determined that you are a very loving individual who's been thinking and believing just the opposite. No matter what you've done for others, you always seem to see yourself in an unloving light. Kids, relatives, and even your spouse repeatedly tell you things that align with the idea that you're unloving, reinforcing it as your truth. However, this is not the truth! You are pure love. God has made you that way, and it is just some silly programming based on events when you were very young that caused you to believe that you're unloving. It's not what they're saying that spells out this unloved conversation for you, but the filter—the little voice in your head that filters their remarks and interprets them to mean that you're unloving. In truth, you are probably the most loving and self-sacrificing person around. This becomes a real part of your own personal dilemma because you believe yourself to be unloving and therefore work overtime in order to support your identity and selfhood for proving you *are* lovable.

You're like a hamster on a wheel, running and moving and doing for others as fast as you can. You become resentful and wounded when those closest to you say things you consider to be statements of how unloving or inadequate they think you are or how bad a nurturer you have become. You begin to believe that they're lying because they want something. The frustration that results is enormous, but you don't question them, fearing that your filtering may be right, and you really are unloving.

What's really happening is that you're hearing/filtering the same validating conversations over and over, day after day. You are seeking evidence to validate the programming you received when you were young. The mind seeks to prove its belief systems by manipulating your thoughts and all contrary information to conclude that you are unloving.

Though this seems somewhat twisted, it makes the mind feel like everything is fine and that life as you know it is right and true. The ego spends a great deal of time and energy to stay connected to what is familiar, even if it can be harmful to you.

You might ask yourself how you got this way. Although the *how* is not really that important in this case, it may be as simple as some authority figure in your life wanting a hug when you were young. You might have been too busy being a child at that moment to stop and comply with their wish. Suddenly, they decided to tease, like many adults do, saying, "Aww Beth, you don't want to give Aunt Sandy a hug? YOU are going to make Aunt Sandy very sad!" Though they were playing with you, you may have taken it as an accusation that you were unloving, or they may have even called you unloving in an effort to manipulate you into giving them a hug. They might have even pretended to cry and say how sad you were making them. This sort of thing happens all the time. As a child, we are uncertain of how to actually interpret these events using the little information and framework we have. In that very moment, you may have been too involved with something and didn't want to stop, maybe even busy filling a diaper, but because Aunt Sandy didn't get a hug, you will have a complex for the rest of your life. This may sound strange and elementary, but it is very true, and in far too many cases.

Aunt Sandy just wanted some attention and didn't mean any harm, but as a young, very impressionable child you became imprinted with the idea that you were unloving. You were left with a shocking idea that now prompts you to seek constant validation of this belief about yourself for years on end. Nearly everything and everyone in your life, from the people you hung around with as a teenager to those you dated and eventually married, have all somehow been in alignment with certain beliefs about yourself, and this is one of your beliefs. Now, you stand tall and know beyond a shadow of a doubt that you are an unloving. Deep inside, you know it's not true because you're so sensitive and full of feelings and have so much passion pent up and just pleading to get out. You're sure that you express it, but it doesn't seem to make any waves according to your interpretation of the feedback that you get.

Well, relax—I am here to tell you that if you ask the key people in your life at the right time, when things are calm and smooth, they will tell you how much they love you and how appreciative they are of everything that you do. They will tell you that your actions and the things you do for them every day demonstrate loving, loud and clear. Then they'll tell you about how you come across to them at other times. These are manifestations of the way you feel, based on the belief that you're not loving. In order to validate this as a truth, there are some characteristics that you have embodied and probably adopted along the way. Listen and watch closely for them, because awareness of these very characteristics can serve to shift your entire presence in a way that ensures no one ever sees you in that light again.

To effectively do this without a good coach, a good facilitator, and/or a great workshop, you should probably be engaged in a lot of journaling. Write down all your feelings on this and work your way through it. In fact, it's what I do myself when things come back up for me at times. It is in these writings that you should begin to affirm that you are a loving person and a divine child of Spirit, made perfect and whole in every way. You should write and acknowledge that you are perfect in every way because you are the absolute perfect expression of yourself the way that was intended at every moment in your life. You are a divine manifestation of love and spirit, and no one and nothing can take that away from you. You are because you are, and you need no further validation to confirm your existence in this world, in your family, or in the community in which you live and operate.

The reason you can be the most honest with people that you don't know is because you have very little at stake. A great example of this is socializing via the World Wide Web—with little invested and little to lose, people are able to be much more honest than they can with those they're close to. With normal relationships, you have a sizable investment because people know you to some extent, even if your risks are managed well. This creates a certain fear of losing these relationships or a fear that they can hurt you with information you share. They have a hold on you in some way. This is the fear that keeps us from truly being ourselves and maintaining real intimacy with the people closest to us. Despite this, once you have declared yourself as whole and repaired the denied aspects of self, the insecurities leave and you are able to be open and honest without the fear of losing the ones you love and care about. This is the true gift of knowing yourself at this level and declaring yourself as being whole and complete, with all aspects of Self intact.

MOVING FORWARD

- chapter twenty -

The Art of Flow is nothing more than a system of efficient co-creation. Whether you look at yourself as creating or co-creating, what matters is the fact is that you are accountable to every aspect of your life.

I know this can be a scary proposition for all of us, but the sooner you can embrace this, the more quickly you can begin creating the life you desire. That's the great truth that this book holds for all of us. The tools have been provided, and now it is up to us to put them to work to build a happy, joyous life free from lack, pain, and suffering.

Every single self-help and spiritual book on the market is pushing for us to accept ourselves completely. Once this happens, nothing can hold us back from living the life we've been longing for deep inside. Our biggest issues lie in self-criticism and limited beliefs about our lives. To get beyond these into a state of true self-acceptance and seeing the perfection in life at every turn is a tremendous catalyst that can catapult us into a life of freedom.

For many years now, I've heard people sell the idea of freedom in every form and area of focus, but in truth there is only one freedom—the freedom that happens within us. This book contains those elements that contribute to real freedom, and I want to summarize them for you now.

Life is a river; it's fluid, ever-changing, and always moving. If we allow the river to carry us, we will remain in constant motion and good things will come to us as we float along. This is a fabulous way to live, though not an easy task to maintain. Along the way, we watch the scenery evolve and latch on to things because we desire them, like them, or are afraid of living without them. When this happens, all sorts of breakdown begin to occur.

We are meant to live in a fluid state. We are born into this world through fluid. The vast majority of our physical make-up is fluid. When we learn to embrace fluidity, our lives seem to work out better than the times we attempt to force good things to happen. This means that fluid change is our inherent state of being and to get there, we need to just let go and stop battling the current.

People focus a lot on the need to be flexible, but flexibility implies a certain tension in the system—you're either living in an undesired state or pushing yourself to keep going, even though you feel otherwise. Consider a branch on a tree; you can flex it or lock it into position, but eventually it will lose some of its strength, start to fray, or even snap. For us, this implies continuous stress. In contrast, fluid does not bend, constrict under tension and stress, or break under pressure. It exists and adapts. Fluid does not insist on the details determining the route to its destination; it always takes the path of least resistance. Fluid moves freely or sits quietly without tension. Its relationship to nature is one of harmony in keeping with surrounding conditions, capable of both life-giving serenity and powerful force.

When we embrace the concept of fluidity, we are embracing the power of peace, harmony, and strength. There is nothing weak about living in fluid motion. In fact, it takes great inner discipline and strength to do so. To willingly live in constant motion and change takes great courage, but the benefit is to live without stress and tension.

To me, the concept of space is the most important principle in this book. When you understand how to create the space you seek, the river of life will absolutely draw you together with what you desire. Bear in mind though, that the space must be clear and clean, and it must be prepared in such a way that it will not attract according to past patterns, events, or situations. The space created must match that which is desired, and all baggage must be cleared to allow new things to move freely into your new way of being.

The principles of flow are nothing less than the most powerful tools for us to clear the space in our minds. If you don't willingly prepare the space, the Universe will take over by creating situations forcing you to deal with the baggage. That may seem counterintuitive, but I've seen it happen again and again in the lives of many people. In other words, resistance to change can bring about even more difficulties until you let go and clear the way.

If you stay the course, I can assure you that after the tumultuous waters subside, there will have been a shift significant enough to create the space needed for your intention. This isn't always easy for people to understand. Just remain accountable for everything going on and realize it is a reflection of the baggage that needs to be cleared before your paradigm rearrangement can occur. Think of it like an engine—you cannot produce energy without burning fuel. Elementally, you have to give something up to achieve the power you seek. In the same way, you must almost always give up something — either willingly or by force — to receive that which you seek.

It's also critical to become more aligned by reclaiming aspects of yourself and circumventing your sabotage mechanisms. While these are important to understand, there is little that we can do on our own. This is where including others in your process is essential. In the Art of Flow, we offer Flow Coaching in person, by phone, and online for those interested in furthering these principles in their life. We also provide support through online groups, webinars, tele-seminars, and workshops. We suggest you plug into the Art of Flow Community with us and utilize all of the recordings, videos, and services we provide. Our goal is for you to be a powerful creator of your life, living a life of peace and harmony.

If you are unable to join us in the Art of Flow Community, my suggestion for you is to study this book with a group. If you can't find one, start one! Explore the depth of the concepts that have been revealed and do the processes, both individually and as a group. Be accountable to the group for your results, and I promise you will begin to see the stream of flow in action.

If the above suggestions aren't suitable for your situation, the next step is to find a seminar, workshop, or local spiritual group (like the Unity Church) to connect with. If, for whatever reason, you are unable to connect with us and the rest of the Art of Flow Community, these people can be invaluable to your process.

May the world feed you pearls of wisdom and your entire journey be filled with peace, harmony, and living your bliss.

Namasté

ABOUT THE AUTHOR

Freddie Zeringue has been a transformational breakthrough coach and workshop facilitator for 25 years. His workshops and one-on-one coaching have long been noted for the dramatic, positive shifts that participants and clients achieve in the areas of health, relationships, prosperity, and general well-being. Often, all they needed was that extra level of insight in order to embrace lives that reflect the fullness they've always longed for.

Freddie has been the Publisher of *Natural Awakenings Magazine — Northeast Florida* for more than 11 years and was instrumental in designing the Natural Awakenings Publishing Corporation's National Media Sales Program. Natural Awakenings is the largest natural health/holistic living magazine in the country.

In addition to his background in natural health, publishing, and marketing, Freddie is trained in Ontological Design (the study of Being), Hypnotherapy, and Advance Communications.

CPSIA information can be obtained at www.ICGtesting.com
Printed in the USA
LVOW08s1116211114

414937LV00010B/144/P